The Shaman's Tree

Awakening to the
Everyday Miraculous

/

The Shaman's Tree

*Awakening to the
Everyday Miraculous*

ROBERT HOFFMANN M.A.

A message of hope for our world at a crossroads

WOOD HORSE PRESS
Kingston New York

WOOD

HORSE
PRESS

Published by Wood Horse Press
an Imprint of Rinchen Publications
20 John Street
Kingston, NY 12401
www.woodhorsepress.com
www.rinchen.com

Copyright © 2012 AwakenTrust, LLC
www.awakentrust.com/theshamanstree/

ISBN 978-0-9714554-9-8

Cover and interior design by Naomi Graphics
www.naomigraphics.com

Dedication

May any merit generated by the creation of this book be dedicated to the benefit of all beings limitless. May errors or shortcomings of this text be diminished by the intention of its creation and the hope, that we may all arrive at a clear, stable and practical understanding of how to benefit oneself and others without exception. For my own errors and oversights, I humbly ask forgiveness.

"In Shenxi, there is a flower nestled softly between
the temple Ao and the river Yun.
So much of this began with the beauty there."
- From "The Magic Flower," by Robert Hoffmann M.A. (unpublished)

Contents

Disclaimer

Important Notice

The activities and practices set out in this book are documented for educational, informational and/or entertainment purposes only. In using this book and applying the methods within, the reader releases the author, publisher and distributors from liability from any injury, including death that may result.

Shamanic, meditational and martial training can be dangerous-both to the physical and mental health of you and others-if not practiced safely. This book is not intended to replace instruction by a qualified instructor or to substitute for good personal judgment. If in doubt as to the safety of your practice, consult with an expert. You should not attempt self-diagnosis or self-treatment of any kind, nor delay seeking medical treatment, nor embark on any form of mind-body training, including the practices in this book, without consulting your physician before you begin. The publisher, author and distributors of this book do not make any representations or warranties, express or implied, with respect to the information herein. Nothing in this book should be construed as a promise of benefits or of results to be achieved, or a guarantee by the author, publisher or distributors of the safety or efficacy of its contents.

The author, publisher and distributors disclaim any liability, loss or

Acknowledgement

To all of those who have helped me learn, there are not words and time enough to express my gratitude. Though I may fall far below your achievement, may my sincere aspiration honor your efforts.

For tireless support and encouragement, I would like to thank David McCarthy of Wood Horse Press and Naomi Schmidt of Naoimigraphics.com. Special thanks to Melisssa Mandel for her wonderful illustrations. Without your mindful support, this would never have been possible.

All images were used with license from online providers. For full credentials of photos used in this book, please visit: awakentrust.com/theshamanstree

Introduction

*T*here is meaning and purpose in life and that meaning can be known. Discovering the magic of that meaning is the greatest journey we can take, and provides the most complete happiness we can ever enjoy. As we will see, this journey is not an obscure and inaccessible one, available only to mystics in faraway places. It is something we can all experience. It has scientific and artistic dimensions, and is unique to each individual who undertakes it. Above all, it is a path of personal engagement and practice. This journey brings us to the threshold of the absolute. The purpose of *The Shaman's Tree* is to support your journey and your unique discovery of fulfillment. To aid us in this quest, we'll draw from the core shamanic teachings enshrined in the global wisdom traditions.

Every culture, in every age, has honored the rare men and women who could speak the language of nature. This tradition exists still, but is in danger. Historically, speaking the language of nature meant that a person could fulfill his or her destiny while not harming others in the process. Traditionally, the shamans are the masters of this path, although not all who claim mastery have achieved it. Still, shamans have existed in all cultures and at all times. Shamans don't all look the same, and their outer appearance changes as required. Despite the differences, there are underlying principles common to all.

While almost anyone can devise methods for getting what they *think* they want, shamans work differently. Shamans actualize their full potential while not harming the ability of nature, or other people, from doing the same. According to my teachers, this attention to the benefit of oneself and all beings is the greatest gift of the shamans work.

Shamans work to improve the quality of life. Magical plants, sacred incantations, and the fuller functioning of the mind/body represent the essence of shamanic lore. Within this lore are methods for expanding the sensory precision of the body/mind as well as medical and sexual teachings for enriching health. The merit of these teachings has been proven for generations and, increasingly, is being confirmed by modern science. Soon you'll learn proven methods for applying these skills. Whether you skip around, work with one lesson at a time, or read this book straight through, amazing changes can come.

I encourage you to meet the teachers mentioned within. Whenever possible, study from them directly. Many of the teachers you'll read about are getting older, and some have already passed on. There's value in meeting a great teacher, if only for a moment. If it's your destiny, meet them while you can. As you proceed, this book will support your quest along the way. Sweat over this book. Read it often. What you see a year from now will be more than what you find today. Read carefully and apply these teachings to your daily life. Doing so is the famed "vision quest" of old.

"Life's a vision quest," said Master Rick. As if relaying a great secret, he leaned in, looked me square in the eye, and continued, "This quest is based on choice. If we choose well, insight arrives, wonders unfold and we fulfill our destiny. If not, we make life harder than it has to be. Life ain't always easy kiddo, but if we're sincere and don't give up, we've journeyed well." With this advice in mind, let us choose wisely, and let us begin. This book is dedicated to the benefit of all beings everywhere, with gratitude to my ancestors, my teachers, and the source of existence itself.

HOW TO USE THIS BOOK

Feel free to read the book straight through, or open it randomly and work with whatever you find. This book is less like a manual and more like a series of vignettes helping us reflect on the quality and composition of the life we live. Here you'll find helpful tools and strategies on how to get the most out of your gifts. What you get out of them though, is based on choice – so choose wisely.

This book is organized into three sections. The first of these deals with the foundations of shamanism. It has five essays describing the worldview common to most of our global wisdom traditions. In essence, part one introduces the basic elements of the shaman's tool kit. Familiarity with this tool kit will assist you in your shamanic quest for vision.

This section provides a reference point for the material provided in the second and third sections.

Section Two offers examples of how skillful shamans have

applied their knowledge in meeting life's problems. It delivers concrete, real life examples on the essence of the shaman's path. Applying this information, you'll be able to consider how you may address some of the challenges you face. Finishing section two, you should be inspired and begin to identify ways you may actualize your deeper potential.

Section Three offers what can be called a "basic training" in essential shamanic skills. It provides you with instructions on how to develop these skills, which will be of great help no matter which path of study you travel.

I cannot speak for all shamanic paths, or all shamanic schools. However, the masters I've met all advocate one single teaching on which the rest depend. That one teaching concerns our relationship to wholeness and full potential. Shamanism is about expressing that potential. Insight on that potential is spread all throughout this book, and treated from different perspectives. While we won't deal with that crucial teaching just now, this much can be said. According to my instructors, if we maintain an open heart, respect life, and do our best to support the benefit of all beings, not only will we discover the master key of high quality shamanism, but we'll come very close to the meaning and purpose of life itself.

With such a noble purpose in mind and such a natural path before us, let's get to it!

4

PART ONE

Foundations

*Core Insight on the
Essence of Being Human*

WE ARE ALL SHAMANS

"When you see the leaves turned upside-down, the white side turned to the sky, you know a storm is coming." "How do you know?" I asked incredulously. With a warm smile, my mother said, "Because your grandfather told me so. He knew a lot about the weather. She continued, "Since my childhood, whenever I've seen this happen, it's always rained, or come real close." It seemed like magic to me. Within the hour, the sky darkened, and the warm summer air let loose. "Raining cats and dogs," as my mom would say. It seemed like magic – my mother could see "hidden causes."

Now, years later, I've seen enough to know that when a storm's coming, there are telltale signs. And in fact, some trees do turn their leaves upside-down as a storm approaches. As a "mature scientist," I know there's a "tree" reason for this behavior – but from a child's point of view, the one I most easily remember, the turning of the leaves is a secret message. It is a message not everyone knows how to read, but my grandfather did know. And much of that knowledge he passed down to his daughter, and then later, through my mother, to me. I was an infant when my grandfather died, but I've come to learn he was much more a shaman than I ever knew.

Shamanism is the intersection of materiality with the wisdom of living life holistically. For this reason, some people think that shamanism is "opposed" to material existence. Nothing could be further from the truth.

Shamanism is not a rejection of the predictable movements

of existence. Nor is it a rejection of science. In fact, authentic shamanism is very scientific and science, in essence, comes from the shamanistic. Before science spoke, the shaman listened. We owe much of modern science to the shaman, and we would be better off if we remembered it. Amidst the intersection of science, faith, intuition, and learning, the shaman waits.

Shamanism is very cerebral, but at the same time, it's very emotive – very sensual – it must be so. "A well balanced shaman is a well-balanced man," said Master Rick. "Or, a well-balanced woman," I added. Master Rick smiled, nodding in agreement.

Shamanism is an expression of balancing life, and just like any other effort, the quality of your intention affects the results. Read that again! The quality of your intention affects the results. We are thinking and feeling beings. Our level of thought and feeling are important in creating the quality and composition of human life. This is the "transmutation" of the old alchemy, and good alchemy begets good results. Some results are obvious; others reside silently in the heart, enriching life from behind the scenes.

You and I contend with the exact same forces as the shaman or shamaness. Matter, time, and space are the field upon which we all play. We are all shamans whether we know it or not – and for those willing to accept the premise, wonders abound.

BUTTERFLY WINGS

Shamanism has two wings. One is the wing of grace; the other is the wing of choice. The relative importance of one wing or the other depends on the way the wind blows. The two wings come together in the body/mind of the student. The body/mind is the connection between grace and the activities of the will.

When the two wings work properly, in harmony with structure and function, we live, love and learn. When one or both of the wings become misshapen or laden with burdens not required, flight becomes unstable. As a result, we wind up flying in circles, often a downward spiral. Thankfully, owing to the power of spirit, there's a way to adjust. If we balance our choices in harmony with the wholeness of life, we can improve our flight.

"Butterflies go from the top of the world to the bottom," said a Tuskegee medicine man. "But they don't do it on their own. They travel light. Butterflies work, but equally rely on Grandfa ther's (Creator's) wind. That's how butterflies can fly much farther than anything else. They use no-force and always seem evanescent. They are welcomed and provide joy wherever they go."

THE SHAMAN'S TOOL KIT

Shamans cooperate with nature in an effort to support the fullest harmony possible. Specifically, they make use of hygiene, posture, breath, awareness, medicinal herbs and energy exchanges to support personal and global wellness. The many schools of shamanism have developed unique tools for enhancing balance. Each school of shamanism developed specialized approaches for balancing life based on the time and place in which they lived.

Despite the differences among shamanic schools, all activities arise from either the action of grace or the activity of the shaman. The nature of the results achieved depends on how well our actions align with the harmony of which we are a part. According to the masters, all human action highlights the interplay between personal activity and the grace of existence. These are the two "wings" introduced in Chapter 2. The chart below shows the essential elements of the shaman's tool kit. The first four items belong to the wing of personal action; the last one emerges from the wing of grace.

Method	Function
Methods of Physical Hygiene	Dress, diet and detoxification to optimize healthy functioning of the body
Methods of Movement	Exercises designed to dredge and clear physical and energetic linkages between organ systems
Methods for Learning	Pathways and states of mind to access the effective wisdom held within traditional culture
Methods to Interact with Environmental Energies	These methods allow a clear interaction between environmental bio-electric functions and those of the human body.

We all have a natural connection to the shaman's tool kit. The only difference is that the shaman is deeply aware of this connection and strives to enhance the fullness of that connection in each and everything he or she does. A good example of this can be found with the breath. "Everyone breathes," said Master Rick, "but not everyone breathes with the full measure of life. With one breath you can change your world. When the breath is complete and in harmony with conditions, it is then that your vision and you become one."

Finding our vision usually happens bit by bit. Rarely does the entirety of a life's vision unfold all at once. For that reason, the tools of the shaman are used to adjust our alignment, so that our natural flow – our full potential – may synchronize with the ever available connection with Grace. Utilizing the shaman's tool kit we clarify our link with Grace, help others do the same and then step by step – express our highest purpose. Precise methods for working with the shaman's toolkit will be provided throughout this book.

ELEMENTAL QUALITIES

*A*ll schools of shaman-
ism recognize the
undeniable link between humanity and the natural world.
Understanding the significance
of that interconnection, the shamans made that interconnection the
focus of everything they did. The reasons are clear – everything is
connected. The opposite of this connection is rigidity and tension, a
forcible separation of things that only makes life harder – both here
and in the worlds beyond.

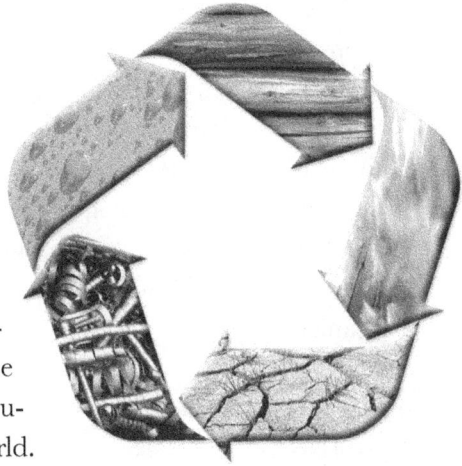

To embody and communicate interconnection in their communities, shamans created sophisticated ways of helping people
live in harmony with that interconnection. A powerful tool in that
regard is the "five elements" model. Different schools have different names for the "five elements," but the meaning is remarkably
similar. Here we'll use the five elements model because it's easy and
accurate.

The elemental model of life encodes profound spiritual and
scientific truths. Almost any activity in life can be understood
through the lens of this model. Typically, the elements are described
as Metal, Fire, Wind, Water and Earth. Although the descriptions
below are common, there are variations. Bear in mind that when
people are truly natural, no model is required. Nonetheless, especially at the beginning, models can be helpful.

Metal often refers to our connection with grace, or the highest purpose. Fire represents the state of mind. Wood (some models say Wind), represents the process of observing patterns, learning, and timing. Water represents following and using resources appropriately. Earth refers to the shape or the method used to address a particular problem. Taken together, the five elements model provides a powerful way to address the complexity of life's challenges.

The five elements combine easily with the shaman's tool kit. Let's revisit the shaman's tool kit, applying the five element model to its organization.

Method	Function
Methods of Physical Hygiene - Earth	Dress, diet and detoxification to optimize basic cellular functions.
Methods of Movement - Water	Exercises designed to dredge and clear physical and energetic linkages between organ systems.
Methods for Learning - Wood	Pathways and states of mind to access the effective wisdom held within traditional culture.
Methods to Interact with Environmental Energies - Fire	Allow a clear interaction between environmental bio-electric functions and those of the human body based on ones state of mind.
Methods to Promote Fuller Reliance on Grace - Metal	Methods for maintaining a specific mindset which promotes a fuller relationship to grace, by fostering a clear conscious connection with the ever-present grace that creation makes available to all who will receive it.

As you can see, the elemental representation of life provides a comprehensive but simple view of life. Any problem can be managed by considering how to bring the five elements into balance. Examples of how we might use these powerful ideas for improving our lives are offered all throughout this book.

THE THREE GATES

Shamans identify three types of experiences which impact our alignment with the meaning and purpose of life. The three types of experiences are often called "Methods of the Three Gates" or "Three Phases." In brief, the three gates involve the body, mind and spirit. The three gates often interact, and distinctions between them are not always clear. Nonetheless, most activities tend to be more aligned with one gate or the other. Depending on the situation, shamans may combine gates, or work with one gate on its own. Either way, harmony begets harmony. In fact, whether methods are combined or not, is of less importance than whether or not a method will promote harmony under a given set of circumstances. The following examples shed more light on the properties of the three gates.

The three gates support and interact with one another. Accordingly, work in one gate necessarily helps to improve the balance and function of all the gates. In addition, at birth, each one of us is born with some level of activation in one or more of the three gates. What is often called "talent" or "propensity" may be attributed to the degree to which one or more of the gates may already be open. Despite the fact that we all have natural skills in the three gates, developing those skills requires systematic training. For example, the beginning student must achieve a certain minimal level of stability in the Body Gate before methods of the Mind or Spirit Gate are taught. Each school manages this process differently, but the guidelines are the same. With this in mind, let us consider the three gates.

THE BODY GATE

The shaman contends with powerful energetic forces. It is important that the shaman healthfully manage the interaction of those energies. The body is a structure through which mental, physical, and spiritual forces flow. Activities which support good hygiene are of benefit. Hatha yoga, shapeshifting, Tai Chi, as well as overtly physical acts all fit into the category of the body gate. Body gate methods benefit the body directly and promote harmony of the mind and our connection with spirit.

THE MIND GATE

Methods of the mind gate promote concentration and connect the dots between spiritual realities and their corresponding physical structures. An example of this is how a skillful Chi Gung Master will develop meridian power. "In the beginning, you must know that energy exists," said Master Shih. He continued, "Once you do, then you study with a teacher who will show you how it moves. With your own concentration and study, you'll understand patterns, and will understand the classical medical texts." That study would be like the application of the mind gate.

SPIRIT GATE

The Spirit gate is beyond words, but words may approximate. A word that comes close to the Spirit Gate is "Grace." Forgiveness comes from Grace. Recognizing that human life is not manmade and that we often tend to do things that go against wellness, shamanic practices should promote an unobstructed relationship with Grace, the source of existence. The result of that relationship is an ego in balance with wholeness. Proper alignment of the ego is essential. The ego is often affected by environmental challenges, mental turmoil, or physical hardship. As a result, the mind-body may be fettered with conflicted thoughts or bodily imbalance. Because of this, the link with grace may appear unstable. Aware of this connection, the shaman refines all the gates to improve the quality of our availability to Grace. Grace is all powerful and may intercede at any moment and under any conditions. Nonetheless, the shaman, ever mindful of the unity of existence and thankful for life itself, humbly works the three gates to honor and permit an easy and welcomed relationship with grace.

SYNERGY AND THE SHAMANIC ROOT
Wholeness Embodied

Shamanism reveals synergy. Life is synergy. Synergy means that everything is connected and that the whole is greater than the sum of the parts. For example, the scent of your beloved is more than a chemical formula. The taste of your favorite food is more than the organic compounds creating it. All of this is a kind of information. There is meaning in information. Life's events dance meaning in the theater of context. Shamanic work allows us to make the most of each moment, because we understand its connection to the context, to the whole.

The Three Gates and the Five Elements present a map of the basic pattern of wholeness. This wholeness is the core of the shamanic process, also called the shamanic root. We express this wholeness when we apply our intelligence to harmonizing with the fullness of nature. After all, it is nature which bore us. We are the children of nature, despite the persistent illusion that we may rebel in separation.

Human life is a microcosm of the universe. We are made of the same fundamental stuff – living intelligence included. The entire universe is intelligent and alive; it can be no other way. The sooner you realize this, the better.

The Three Gates and the Five Elements provide a reference point for addressing our shamanic root. Generally speaking, the shamanic root involves balancing five elemental expressions in harmony with life. The five expressions are: hygiene, physical potential, mental potential, application of potential (in work and relationships), and finally, faith in the intelligent substance of existence, which some call God. The three gates, five elements and the shamanic root accord with the treasured knowledge of every wisdom tradition. No matter what tradition you follow, this information can serve you well.

Keep in mind that a given circumstance is never the sole property of one element. The gates and elements are used as a reference, not an absolute definition. In life, you will find overlap and nuance. It's like jazz. You learn the scales, but the changes are endless. Correct change promotes creativity and allows life to remain fresh, vital and dynamic. There are innumerable possibilities in each and every day; there are unlimited ways to fulfill your destiny in harmony with the fullness of life.

As you move along, you'll find clues as to how the masters categorized experience. Consider how their classification may be of benefit to you. Use the examples provided to connect with a deeper understanding of the dynamic, holistic way that shamans face life's challenges. Bit by bit, you'll discover a sophistication that is natural, basic, but often lost in our linear clock-fixation. Recover the knowledge of spheres and cycles. Ironically, linearity will be balanced by this approach. Although shamanic, non-linear thinking is quite the rage these days, it's only one half of the whole. Both are required. Although thinking "out of the box" is a modern catch phrase, the shamans have been thinking out of the box for eons. Riding on their coat-tails, let's give it a shot too!

GRACE AND THE
ORGANIZATION OF THIS BOOK
A Summary of Part One

*B*y now, it should be clear, we're all shaman. We all work with the same basic forces and we're made of the same basic stuff. The only difference is that the shamans know what's going on, in the fullest sense. The rest of us live life like confused actors unaware of the stage directions. If we just open up to our full potential, we will see.

The quality of our shamanism depends on how well we harmonize with nature and how fully we balance our hearts. Examples of how we might approach that harmony are included all throughout this book. I hope these true accounts will inspire you to greater harmony.

The shaman's journey is a discovery of how our human lives emulate and fit into the balance of nature. The journey of discovery is rooted in choice. We have the free will to harmonize with life, or destroy the harmony on which we depend. We literally choose how we want to learn and live. No matter how we choose though, the lessons are always the same, and the way we approach them must always be creative. Despite the truth of our free will, we must never forget that we cannot be separate from the wholeness of nature which sustains us. A compassionate respect for interconnection is the fundamental ethic of existence. Without this awareness, life becomes a play of fear, manipulation and greed. In short, when we divorce ourselves from wholeness, we live life from the most limiting parts of ourselves. And from there, we cannot express our full potential, nor enjoy the meaning and purpose of life.

The three gates are the pathways through which we interact with the five elements of the natural world. The three gates and five elements are simple models used to effectively engage the quantum reality of our existence. This quantum reality hinges on choice. Managing our choices wisely, we expand potential and honor the cycles of life on which we depend. By contrast, poor choices make life more difficult than it has to be. No matter when we start, the moment we catch the mind in process and begin to improve, improvement comes. As the old saying goes, "an inch of practice, an inch of skill."

This first section of our journey has provided a context for our travels. A context is a platform for organizing ideas and action. Everything is a context, so choose your relationship to context wisely. Now, with the basics laid out, we can move on.

Part two of this book provides examples of how the masters and everyday people have addressed challenges while celebrating successes with the three gates and the five elements. There are similarities and differences in the approaches you'll find. I encourage you to study the fundamentals as you marvel in the differences.

The examples from part two will give you a conceptual framework you can use to engage and balance the powerful emotions you're sure to encounter. These stories remind us to stay positive even when times are tough. No good effort is wasted. Use these stories as a basic map for discovering the miraculous in the outside world and inside of your own life.

True Stories of Insight and Inspiration

The Dynamic Worldview of the Shaman

YOU'RE LUCKY YOU'RE SOFT

"You're lucky you're soft, Robert. If you weren't soft, then this would be difficult to heal." I went to Master Liu's office for help with a painful stiffness in my back. Over the years, this stiffness would come and go, but when it came, it was bad. One afternoon, while working on a cattle farm in Upstate New York, the pain was so bad I had to lay down right in the middle of a field and wait till it passed. Well, it never did. I went home that night stunned as to where this pain came from. It took three or four days for the pain to subside, and I lived in fear of its return. I hadn't met Master Liu yet. Looking back, I wonder how things may have been different if I had met her earlier.

Years later, same pain. Master Liu led me into her treatment room and began the questioning. "Show me every place that hurts, and then find the exact point, with your finger, where the pain comes from." It was an odd way to ask the question, I thought. "What do you mean, the exact point," I asked, "it hurts everywhere." "No!" she answered gruffly. "Each pain has a seed. Show me where the seed of the pain is, the root." Baffled, and a bit put off, I did my best. I showed her where the pain radiated to and then with my best guess, showed her the "seed" of pain, as she called it.

Without delay, she began her treatment. Within minutes, the pain was gone and did not return. I couldn't believe it. Earlier, on the way to her office, I couldn't even touch my chin to my chest. By the end of the treatment I could touch my toes, bend in any direction and even lift things again. I nearly lifted Master Liu off the ground as I hugged her in gratitude. What she did was nothing short of miraculous.

With a serious but soft voice, she explained how energy blockage can lead to illness. "Illness comes because the energy is blocked. Some blockages happen little by little, others all at once. Either way we should follow nature, and then our health will be as good as possible. The universe always moves its energy, and people should too. When the energy of the Earth does not move, it gets locked up and creates an earthquake. For us, the type of energy blockage determines the effect. One of the best ways to fight off illness is to keep the inner energy strong and to move it in healthy ways." I followed up by asking Master Liu for some basic instructions on how everyday people could help to keep their energy moving.

"One of the best ways is to eat correctly and walk a bit each day. Of course, if you can do more, that's good. Simply patting the body is also good, and it's very easy. But don't misunderstand. If your imbalance is severe, simple patting might not solve the problem. But patting each day can be a way to lessen the severity of symptoms or to solve problems before they come. If something is serious, you must see your doctor, and you must see an expert."

"An expert like you!" I said. Patting me on the shoulder she said, "My master's skill was much better, I just do the best I can." Considering Master Liu's level of skill, the prowess of her master must be awe inspiring.

The next chapter describes the basic method of patting that can be used to support an optimal flow of energy.

THE BENEFITS OF PATTING

*T*he human body is organized along specific lines of electromagnetic force. Asian medicine calls these force lines "meridians." In India, the ancient word for meridian was "nadi." Early Western medicine also recognized the electrical properties of the human body, as did the ancient Africans, Middle Easterners and Native Americans. The electromagnetic reality of the body has been well known for thousands of years.

The Body Electric by Robert O. Becker M.D. details important aspects of the bioenergetic structure of the body. Taking his work as a reference we can understand the truth in what the ancients discovered by spiritual grace and direct experience. We should remember that it is in our nature to know these things directly. The way that the electrical skeleton impacts health is crucial for nderstanding not only the patting exercises, but the sophisticated techniques of shamanism as well.

Meridian lines exist on the inside and the outside of the body. Because of this, major organs, viscera, connective tissue and even bones all share an interconnection through energy. Superficial meridians interact and form the major pathways commonly seen in acupuncture textbooks. While there are 20 main channels, the body is enmeshed within thousands of auxiliary meridians large and small. Any of those meridians may be accessed medically to affect specific results.

Because meridian lines originate from and associate with specific organs, it is possible to treat the outside of the body with patting, needles, massage or other therapies in order to promote healthy changes within. Modern Western science is rediscovering these connections with reflexology, trigger point therapy, and chiropractic. I call this a rediscovery because the Western medical traditions were largely stripped of their holistic medicine during the Dark Ages and the Scientific Revolution. Since then, an aggressive, coarse, and incomplete material science has largely silenced what was ancient, subtle, and refined. Fortunately, quantum science offers some reprieve.

Although simple, patting exemplifies the type of practice that unites the ancient and modern. Western medicine would agree with the gross benefits of patting, and the Eastern viewpoint would acknowledge the superficial while extolling the benefits achieved when we apply the gross with an eye to the subtle. Patting promotes better circulation of blood and lymph, but importantly, helps the body detoxify and balance hormonal secretions. Work sensibly and whenever possible use patting as a warm up, a cool down or as an adjunct to acupuncture, massage, or meditation. The main purpose of patting is to promote a healthy and even flow of energy in all its forms. We'll introduce additional methods of energetic healing in other chapters, but never forget the important lessons and benefits that this accessible, simple method provides.

A BASIC METHOD OF SELF MASSAGE
Patting

*L*oosen the body by gently shaking and wiggling the arms, legs fingers and toes. Roll the head in circles and breathe a few soft deep breaths. Rub your hands, just strongly enough to generate some heat.

Cup your right hand, and begin lightly slapping your left upper chest. Allow your movement to carry your strikes to the inside of your left shoulder and then progressively work down to the palm of the hand. Next, slap the center of the left palm and then begin working your way up the outside of your left arm back to the shoulder. Carry your slapping across the front of your shoulder to your left chest and then the sternum.

Now, let your right arm rest and begin the same pattern, but this time striking the right shoulder and arm. Cup your left hand and begin to slap the inside of the right shoulder, arm and hand in the same way you did the left side.

Now use both hands and lightly slap your chest then abdomen. Allow your hands to arrive at your hips and then slap your hips and then carry downward along the inside of your legs to your ankles. Carry your slapping from the inside of the ankles to the outside of the ankles and then work your way back up the outer thigh. Once you arrive at the outer hip, lightly tap the abdomen a few times. Next rub the kidneys in a V shape with the backs of the hands. Perform the kidney rub three, six, nine or twenty-seven times.

Now, rub your hands together and run your fingers through your hair from the forehead to the back of the neck. Do this three

times. Once finished, massage the face, ears and neck lightly with fingers making gentle circular strokes. When you are finished, let your hands rest comfortably at the abdomen, breathe deeply three times and sit in peaceful quiet until you are ready to exit the practice. Repeat this method as much as you like.

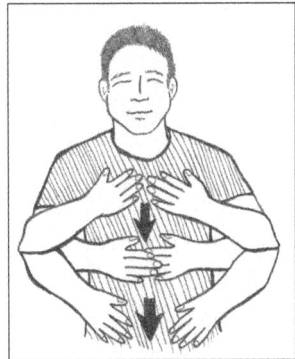

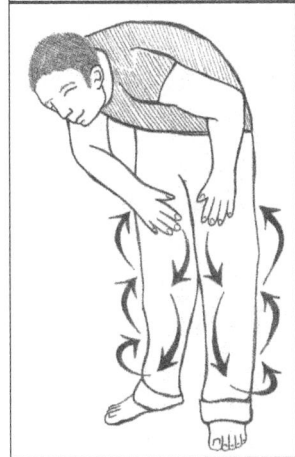

SEEING WITH YOUR PALMS

"I learned from her that I had 'eyesight' in the palms of my hands; that I could read 'enexrgy' with them; that I could use the power of my hands to ward off invisible dangers or rid myself of unwanted negative influences."

– Jose Stevens PhD, on the power of hands in
Central Mexican shamanistic practices

Hands – almost nothing represents humanity more completely than the shape and power of our hands. By power, we mean transformative capacity.

Our hands lack the powerful grip of the Great Primates and the load-bearing strength and combative prowess of the larger mammals. However, the human hand with its opposable thumb sets us apart from the rest of existence. This unique characteristic has been celebrated by indigenous peoples since antiquity.

The development of human culture owes much to the power of our hands. With our hands, we have been able to develop tools, use those tools and use our hands to form bonds between people. Hands may be used to build, love, heal, and destroy. No other species on this planet has the creative and destructive capacity of humanity. So much of that power rests in the palm of our hands.

Beyond the structure of our hands, there is a subtle anatomy. This anatomy was known to the ancients and modern science, and is beginning to re-emerge. The ravages of the last Ice Age all but decimated our connection with pre-historical information on the miraculous, energetic anatomy of the human body. Modern science has recently developed the tools required to scratch the surface of understanding. Thankfully, the shamanic custodians of ancient knowledge will teach us, if we are willing to learn. It is by their influence that humanity has a chance of making it through these turbulent times.

Master Stevens speaks about "seeing with the palms." This sight is a global observation. In the Near East, the palm was depicted with an eye in its center. It was called the "seeing, feeling eye of the hand." Judeo-Christian art depicts the prophets and saints as blessing the faithful using the center of the palm. In Asia, the center of the palm is reputed to contain a powerful energetic enter, called "Lao Gong," in Chinese. Lao Gong, or the "Palace of Labor," is just that – a place wherein wondrous work and wondrous results reside.

Steven's grandmother spoke about the Wirrarika of Central Mexico, and how they would use the center of the palm for detecting infirmity as well as ridding the body of unwanted energetic influences. In Asia, the center of the palm is used to bless and relieve a person of energetic disease. It is a compelling fact that, all over the world, native shamans speak of the power of the "eye" in the palm.

Massage your hand frequently. Let the hand be relaxed and free of stiffness. Master T.K. Shih offers a wonderful course on how to use your hands for healing the body. If you can, take the opportunity to learn from this rare and remarkable man. Learn about the Lao Gong and use it to build wonders in your life.

DREAMING WITH PLANTS

"That night, I had the strangest dream. In the dream, I saw a green spear sticking upright out of the ground, surrounded by scintillating yellow hues. The yellow colors seemed to be flowers, but also looked like waves of light traveling up and down the green spear. I didn't know what to make of it. The next day, my padrino (spiritual guide), came to my house and presented me with mullen. I didn't know what mullen was before my padrino came by that morning. When I saw the mullen he carried, I recognized that mullen was the plant I had seen in my dream the night before."

— A practitioner's tale about his messenger plant

*P*lants deserve more credit than we give them. Genetically, they've been around for billions of years longer than us, and the memories they carry in their DNA are astonishing. But plants appear odd. They appear to be silent. They appear to be immobile and they don't appear to be intelligent. Appearances can be deceiving.

Luther Burbank, George Washington Carver and Deepak Chopra are but a few who cite instances where the intelligence of plants is implied if not proven. At the very least, the ground consciousness inherent in all existence possesses unique attributes when organized in plant form. Therefore, plants express the consciousness field around them, harmonizing with it, augmenting whatever the ambient field may be. Alternately, plants are self-conscious in their own way (the perspective I abide by), and are willing to harmonize with good people when possible, but may be unable to resist the strong will of bad intentions issued by those with malefic intentions. Nonetheless plants, as with all things, are united with the dynamic web of existence. As such, whenever possible, their inner urge is to harmonize with balanced potential, not restrict it. Dreaming with plants can be a powerful ally in striving for insight and healing.

METHOD

Take a walk in the park, or anywhere there's an abundance of flora. As you walk, pay attention to the plants you see, especially the ones you see and hear! When you intuitively recognize a plant that is seeking you, go to it. Stand near it, approach it carefully – some plants withdraw consciousness as quickly as they send it out. Some plants need to be coaxed.

When you have established a connection with a plant that speaks with you, spend time understanding its history – ask it questions – listen for responses. At the right time, ask if you may take a leaf or branch with you. If the answer is yes, leave a few drops of water, grains of rice or seed as payment and take a piece of the plant with you. Be careful not to damage it to the point it might die. On the other hand, if the plant indicates you may not take a piece of it with you, it's not a rejection. The two of you might not be ready. Alternately, maybe the plant feels it's best for you to work with its medicine "as it is." Either way, listen to the plant – it is sharing its energy with you. At night, place the leaf or branch under your pillow. Fall asleep thanking the universe for this gift and listen for the messages of the plant as you sleep. If the plant is safe to eat, make a tea or hold a tiny bit of it in your mouth as you sleep. The results can be amazing. Many practitioners have found this to be an amazing source of insight and inspiration. Enjoy.

TINA,
THE PERUVIAN SHAMANESS

She fools you. She might be the curator of a small spiritual shop, or she might be that sweet woman you bump into at the bakery – but a shaman? No, she couldn't be. But she is.

She once told me about a particularly difficult man in her life, a business associate. He was constantly arguing with her, setting up barriers to her advancement, just because he liked to. Once Tina (not her real name), figured out what was going on, all that changed. "Poor thing," she said in a sweet tone, "he didn't even know I was working on him. It really was for his own benefit though. I wasn't doing anything wrong; I was just trying to live my life. Things got better for all of us when he stopped being so obstructive."

She's an emanation of the subtle. Her voice is soft, her gaze softer, but filled with power and integrity. She spoke with an accent both sophisticated and innocent. "There's good work and bad work, Robert." I've seen enough to know the difference. Good work is good for all, and the bad, is bad for everyone. If you do bad work, it's just a question of when it comes back to haunt you."

Many believe it is better to purify karmas in this life rather than trying to deal with them in the afterlife. Indeed, this is one of the advantages of a human life. The astral realms are far too subtle for most. Many a soul gets lost there. The astral states are a challenge for the well prepared – how much more so when the soul is weighed down with the heavy chains of bad karmas yet to be satisfied?

Tina helped me with one of my friends. For months, he was locked in an intractable battle with a neighbor over money that was owed. Typically cool headed, my friend was really getting perturbed by the debt. Discussion was of no use, and the neighbor had no mind of paying the money back. For months, the situation remained in a deadlock. Fearing for my friend's peace of mind, I brought the problem to Tina.

"This should work, it's a very strong 'trabajo' (spell). Use this green candle and burn it once, continuously, until it's all gone. Make sure it's in a safe place, OK? Under the candle, place the name of the person who owes the money. Say the prayer I showed you and, without question, the debt will be paid."

After months of evasion, the debt was paid even before the candle was finished burning. Sometimes what appear as the simplest 'trabajo,' is the most effective. Perhaps the key lay with how the ritual, the intention, and the people involved interact with the correctness of the cause. When a powerful, good intention is brought to bear on a meaningful problem, cosmic forces align, promoting the best possibility of success.

> *"Even if one does not pray to the Gods, if his heart is pure,*
> *will they not come to his aid?"*   – Shobogenzo

SAMADHI
Absorption in Bliss

Yoga is the primary line of Indian shamanism. The sutras of the ancient Indian sage Patanjali are considered the definitive texts of this tradition. Patanjali was very famous in his time, and it is said that he could perform miracles.

The word "sutra" means thread, and the term implies the kind of thing onto which precious items, such as pearls, are strung. The "sutra" is the cord, and the pearls are the bits of information, life-changing information, which, if applied sincerely, will lead to bliss in this life and beyond. However, just as a car can take you from one point to another, but only if you drive it properly, the vehicle of yoga must be used correctly. If you are reckless and foolishly ignore the meaning of the sutras, you'll never reach your destination. You will not only miss the bliss, but you'll encounter more difficulty than would come to you otherwise.

In the sutras, Patanjali describes a state of mind in which the alignment of the body is stable, the emotions are in balance, and the breath is in harmony with what's needed. He describes how the mind may become free of distraction. With this clarity, the mind becomes more powerful and more precise. With this precision, the mind detects feelings, forces, and signs that have always had significance for our lives, but have gone largely unnoticed due to distracting internal chatter and external conditioning. At the right time, says Patanjali, a great peace can wash over the mind. Such peace benefits everyone without exception.

Little by little, the mind turns to the vehicle itself: the body/

mind. This turning and tuning-in is mentioned in all the wisdom traditions and results in exceptional psycho-physical efficiency. It is the vision quest of the Native Americans; it is the "stopping and seeing" of Zen; it is the samadhi of the yogis, and the experience of "Ifaiya" among the Yoruba. All developmental wisdom traditions have a name for this process, despite the fact that, just beyond the name, is the nameless. On the border between subject and object, the seeker becomes mute. Lao Tzu pointed out as much at the very beginning of the Tao Te Ching with the phrase, "the Tao that cannot be spoken."

Meditative absorption (samadhi) may persist for an instant, for hours or even a lifetime, depending on conditions. You may experience occasional flashes of it, or be immersed in it for what appears to be an endless stretch of time. Nonetheless, samadhi itself is just a landmark, albeit an important one. There are ranges of scope and penetration of this state, and the most likely indicator of development of samadhi is the effect in your daily life.

The process of samadhi changes things. When it bears its full fruit, we are no longer able to consider some as near and others as far. Fundamentally, we see the entire universe as an extension of ourselves - *It/We Are/Is.* For this reason, the full development of samadhi exemplifies the phrase, "love others as you love yourself." Miracles, such as healings, levitation and special powers are often attributed to samadhi. Could it be that the potential for unbiased caring for all beings is the greatest effect of all – and the one we now need the most?

THE SAN AND POISONED ARROWS

Once there was a boy who followed the elders and secretly learned the method for making poison. He was careless, as a child often is, and mistakenly rubbed his eye. The poor child died. The shaman was powerless to bring him back. Miracles must work within the structure of life. When we violate the structure of life too greatly, we minimize the window of the miraculous.

*T*he San Bushmen of Africa are probably the oldest continuous culture on Earth. DNA evidence suggests that the San are the direct descendants of some of the first human populations that left Africa more than 100,000 years ago. In San culture, we see a living chain of knowledge reaching back to the earliest times.

In studying the San, I learned of how the San structure the education of their families. Despite the fact that modernization is threatening every aspect of their culture, the San elders maintain a type of education unchanged for generations. Education follows a tradition of apprenticeship, and the requirements of apprenticeship are specific. An example of this is the tribal process of making poisoned arrows for the hunt.

The San, like many shamanistic cultures, believe that knowledge must be shared at the right time. Providing information to a person before they are mature and balanced enough to understand it is considered dangerous. Understanding implies holistic awareness. Knowledge must only be received in proportion to one's experience of the wholeness of life. All too often, an immature mind will use knowledge to secure self-serving and shortsighted goals. Such goals are not only invalid to begin with, but harm everyone from the start. I am reminded of the old Yoruba maxim. "What starts bad usually ends bad." All too often, the shaman are called upon to fix the end result of something that started out bad. Correction is not always possible.

In San culture, it is the men who hunt. For catching big game in the sparse Saharan landscape, poisoned arrow heads are used to fell prey that would be otherwise be untouchable. Many a young man desire the honor of the hunt, but are not taught how to make the poison until they have reached a mature and stable age. Implicit in this custom is the recognition that childhood should be, as much as possible, a time of innocence and a time to be cared for.

Our living ancestors, the San, show that for our lives to succeed – for our heritage to prevail – we must not violate the seasons of living. Information must be shared in keeping with our capacity to manage the responsibility of that knowledge. At the same time, information must not be hoarded. It must be passed on, but done so correctly – in harmony with appropriate timing. It is evidence of illness, not greatness, which dispenses all things to all people regardless of conditions. The shamanic approach is to manage life conditions well, and work responsibly for the benefit of life without corruption or contrivance. Even as we administer the rules, we must follow them. By virtue of their insight, the shamans help us not only to understand when the rules may be bent, but most importantly, why the rules exist in the first place.

DARWIN AND THE SHAMAN'S GOD
PART ONE
The Basics of Natural Selection

*I*n 1859, Charles Darwin published a theory addressing how the many complex forms of life may have arisen. Specifically, Darwin spoke of a formative process called natural selection. According to natural selection, the pressures of survival impact the development of life. Much later on, other scientists came to call this developmental process "evolution." Basically, the idea goes like this.

> *Imagine that there are 100 white moths living in your home town, and only 10 black moths. Now suppose that your town becomes so polluted that all the trees in your area have their bark covered in dark black soot. Well, for the moths that are fond of resting on trees, then the black moths that do so will be much more hidden from their main predators, insects and birds. By extension, any of the white moths who take a rest on those dark-colored trees will "stand out" and become an easier meal. Consequently, when it comes time for "dating and mating," there are likely to be fewer white moths at the party.*

This actually happened. As the industrial revolution swept over Europe, one town in England became famous for the near extinction of its local, white moths. It didn't take long to figure out why. Life conditions (in this case, black soot on trees) influenced which individuals lived long enough to mate. The organisms that successfully mate pass along their family traits. Those family lines that do not mate lose the prospect of having their traits remain in a population as time goes on.

At first glance, natural selection seems to be common sense. What is not common sense, however, is the direction some have taken the basic theory of natural selection. Some scientists use natural selection and many other scientific postulates in order to make a case against the spiritual. They are often the loudest mouths in the bunch, and for that reason many people think that science and spirituality cannot be compatible. If such scientists were only as objective as they claim to be, they would see that scientific truths point exclusively to the holistic quality of mind and matter – that is, straight to the heart of God.

As we shall soon see, the discursive human intellect is not fit for the task of apprehending the *full* meaning and purpose of life. A holistic mind however, is another matter entirely. Darwin said it well…

> *"I cannot pretend to throw the least light on such abstruse problems (i.e. the existence of God). The mystery of the beginning of all things is unsolvable by us."*

If only Darwin was as skilled in relating to the "I" as he was the natural world, he would have discovered one of the shaman's most prized realizations! Significantly, Darwin acquiesced to agnosticism, but not atheism.

DARWIN AND THE SHAMAN'S GOD
PART TWO

Darwin addressed mechanics, not meaning. Furthermore, in his lifetime, Darwin had not met the saints and high-level practitioners. Had Darwin been able to meet authentic masters such as the ones you are finding in this book, I suspect he would have reevaluated certain opinions. Despite his biases, Darwin never closed the book on God, and the tension he perceived between what is called the "secular" and "spiritual" tired him. His journals reflect this.

Had Darwin met an authentic master, he would at least have found greater emotional peace. Before a true master, one cannot but walk away knowing that the sacred and scientific are one, and not in opposition. It's unfortunate that he lost so many years in clouds of emotional confusion. The shaman's path shows us that not only can science and faith complement one another; it can be no other way. As the Brahma Sutra reminds, *"there are not two."* Life is not one and life is not many. Almost sensing the ineffability of these things, Darwin remained pessimistic, but open-minded.

Though he expounded profusely on the mechanics of things, Darwin was remarkably shy on issues of meaning. From the shaman's perspective, the clash, evident in Darwin's writings, indicates that Darwin may have arrived at a very specific shamanic stage. That stage is called, "the dawning of awareness which understands it is both the observer and the observed." The classics say that without a holistic support for this understanding, that is, without enough of a root in the simplicity of life, unfortunate effects result. Essentially, when pressed up against the limits of its own fragmentation, the intellectual mind "short-circuits," and often stagnates in rank materialism, or at best, optimistic agnosticism. Neither should be the final resting place of the precious human mind.

In India, there is a traditional path called Jnana Yoga. "Jna" means, knowledge or information. "Yoga" means union – and indicates bliss. According to the masters of this path, the process of Jnana Yoga is only for those with a heady disposition, those types who like to argue and debate. Few specialize in Jnana Yoga because, as the human mind is so close to the creative, one misstep will lead to arrogant ignorance or a sense that nothing at all can be known. Both lead to unnecessary suffering. The dangers and remedies of jnana practice will be discussed later on.

Discursive intellect is only one ray in the spectrum of awareness. Equally powerful (and relevant) are intuition, emotion, and imagination. I am reminded of Einstein's statement that "imagination is more important than facts." The great scientist Buckminster Fuller would have agreed. For mind to work well, all its rays must have a chance to shine. Favoring one at the expense of others is unwise in life and in the formations of mind. Groening said, "life is not manmade." Darwin said this too. Despite his intuition, Darwin had not learned to keep the "ray" of discursive intellect in balance *enough* to enjoy the implications of that balance. Specifically, when intuition, emotion, imagination and the discursive mind are in balance, we arrive at the bridge between Jnana Yoga and the meaning and purpose of life itself. The bridge will take shape according to the mind in pursuit, but perhaps for the scientist, it might look something like this:

People have consciousness. People are made of atoms.
Consciousness is not separate from existence at any level.
Please feel and understand what this means.

MISFIRE

"He could have killed me. If it wasn't for Jose's work, I'm sure I'd be dead." Pablo (not his real name), spoke in a simple but straightforward way. Even though his life had been on the line, he didn't embellish – he just stated the facts. "Jose's work saved my life." A closer look at the details bears his story out.

Jose had found Pablo at a crossroads of life. Jose was asked to perform a consultation for Pablo, and the consult was given according to Osain, the Yoruba/Congo Lord of the forests and all plants.

"Everything can be done through Osain," said Ifa Oba Nike, a high priest of the tradition and long-time student of the Master. "Osain is the mountain; he is the sacred herbs, and he is the energy shared with us through plant life. Without Osain, life wouldn't exist."

Jose did the consultation and found this man's life to be "twisted." "*Salao*," full of salt, was the phrase he'd use to describe cases like that. He would need sweetness, good luck, something to counteract the salt. The intervention would need to be significant, and it was. There was an offering, and herbs were used as well. Jose said prayers for Pablo, and provided him with an amulet that he would keep with him at all times. The amulet was necessary to maintain *buena suerte*, or "good luck."

A few days later, with the amulet securely in his pocket, Pablo became involved in a terrible fight. The antagonist pulled out a gun and pointed straight for the heart. Pablo, stunned, waited for the worst. Time seemed to slow down, as the assailant's finger squeezed the trigger. Just then, an unmistakable sound filled the air, "click." In the silence, the recognition dawned that the gun had misfired. Quickly, Pablo pushed past the would-be assailant and escaped to safety.

Jose Franz was an Osainista possessing incredible skill. Simple interventions were used for some of the most complex problems, and he wielded his craft with expert efficiency. A native of Santa Clara, Cuba, he had learned the art after he immigrated to America. A Korean War veteran and skilled practitioner of many trades, there wasn't much this man couldn't do, including the magical.

Early in his life, he couldn't have envisioned himself a mystic. But years later, events would see differently. At the appointed time, he became one of the most talented Osainistas I've heard of. I was never able to meet the man, but through his student, much of his wisdom lives on.

TIPPING POINT

For much of the last 500 years, the oft-labeled "objective sciences" have denigrated the shamanic as superstitious self-hypnosis. Often fueled by political, religious or egoistic agendas, shamanic wisdom has faced persecution, scientific derision and the brutalities of book burnings. There remain only vestiges of some shamanic traditions, but fortunately, quite a few remain intact. Putting the pieces together can be of tremendous help to a world in search of a meaningful relationship to its wholeness.

As it emerges from its immaturity, science is finally beginning to see the holographic wisdom encoded in the shamanic. This newfound vision mirrors a larger open-mindedness in society. Overall, such developments are good, but we must be careful. Science is treading on new ground with the shamanic.

Frequently, in the spirit of research, science removes a subject of study from its roots – making it the focus of bright lights and laboratory chambers. Scientists hope to manage variables, but too often they only disrupt synergy. Ironically, it is the presence of variability which adds power to life, as well as shamanic skill.

While both science and shamanism can and should learn from one another, there is a tipping point. If we pull the shamanic too far from its synergy, or remove restrictions from science, both cease to be what they are. The masters say there is a place that unites them both. Shamanism is about that place. That place is the abode of wholeness, regardless of beginnings.

Where will this journey take you? Only you will know.

Nonetheless, the wisdom of the master shamans has enriched my life tremendously, and I hope you will enjoy the same. Balancing science and shamanism by finding what unifies them both, we stand at the gateway to the miraculous.

TALKING TO YOUR TEA

*T*he boy asked me, "What are you doing?" I replied, "Talking to my tea." A quizzical frown blossomed across his face. "Why are you talking to your tea?" His simple question began an hour-long discussion of things that most children his age never think of, but should. I'll try to reproduce the essence of our chat below.

"Have you heard of Masaru Emoto"? (*I knew full well he never had.*) "Well, let me tell you. First of all, he wasn't the only person to discover what I'm going to tell you about, but these days, he's the most famous. Mr. Emoto discovered a way to make beautiful snowflakes."

"What do snowflakes have to do with your tea, Robert?" Shaking his head, eyeballing me with confusion, he turned his head to look at me sideways. "Glad you asked," I answered with a smile.

"Masaru Emoto works with a science called crystallography. Basically, he freezes things and makes them into snowflakes. In fact, if you give Mr. Emoto a piece of rock, he can make that into a snowflake too!" By this point, the poor boy was rolling his eyes as if I were a lost cause.

"C'mon Robert, don't play games." Fortunately, I had my copy of Mr. Emoto's book in my bag. Taking out the book, I walked the boy through the basics.

"Look, when you make things really, really cold, they form

crystals. And then, with a special camera, you take a picture of those crystals and they look like snowflakes. Emoto found out that when you have something like water and you freeze it, the beauty and strength of the snowflakes will change, depending on how you talk to the water.

If I didn't have the pictures in front of me, this boy would have been certain that I was crazy or creating fairy tales. Isn't that interesting... *science and fairy tales, how far apart are they?*

The boy and I leafed through the pages. Sure enough, with time, the boy got the message. Just like Burbank, Carver and Einstein, Emoto had stumbled upon what so many scientists miss, namely, that the attitude you hold affects the results of your life. Whether we are making crystals or making love, how you hold your heart impacts the reality that forms around you.

"Now, look at these pictures here. In these cases, Emoto had people say mean things to the water. And look, the water couldn't make beautiful, strong snowflakes. But then, when people reverse it and say beautiful things, play lovely music and have good intentions, the water is free to create and grow complex, strong crystals. And people are more than 70-percent water. So now you know why I talk to my tea. And I only say nice things. My chi gung Master gave me this tea for healing. I want it to do a good job, so I want the water and the tea to know that I value and appreciate it. That way, the best possible result can occur."

"I'm going to talk to everything, Robert – food, water, even ice cream!" the boy shouted.

"Well, if you're around people who don't know Emoto, you better just think good thoughts. Not everyone has read the book."

"Yeah, I'll probably end up in detention," he said. We both laughed.

UNHELPFUL HABITS

One motivational speaker said "We are the products of our habits." For this reason, many believe that if we improve our habits, we improve our lives. But if we think about it, we may rightfully ask, how do we judge what is an improvement in habit? I asked Master Shi about this important fundamental.

"The life energy in the body wants to flow with nature. Human life comes from nature, so we have to be in harmony with nature, not the other way around." Furiously scribbling notes, I wanted to make sure I took it all in. Suddenly, Master Shi admonished me. "Stop taking notes! That is one of your habits. This is not the time for notes. This is not technical information. If you write notes about it, you will miss it. I'm talking about feeling, about the chi, the life energy. Chi is alive. Your notes are dead. Habits are about chi. If you don't feel it, you will miss it. Listen and feel what I say. The meaning comes from my voice, from the feeling of my experience. The meaning is not just the words. What is carried on the words?" Looking down, he waited for me to release my stranglehold on notebook and pen.

I knew what he was getting at. Oftentimes, a master will teach not by virtue of the words he or she says, but, in fact, the wave-form meaning carried in the spoken word. It's no different than sending positive thoughts to your houseplants and watching them thrive. The written word is not the only form of information. It has taken me a while to really learn that.

To change an unhelpful habit means we have to realign with

the natural flow seeking expression in our bodies/minds. Just as water must pass through rivers and streams, so too must universal energy move through the human body, and pass through for transformation. Unhelpful habits are the signs of a blockage from an earlier time. The seed of a bad habit may have been a mistaken emotion, an accident, trauma, or karma itself.

Conventional psychotherapy attempts to heal unhelpful habits by way of insight. Some feel that approach is inadequate. Psychologist Arthur Janov, for example, points out that the neurotic mind is the same mind as the mind seeking the solution. For that reason, to paraphrase Einstein, "You'll never solve a problem occupying the same state of mind you had when it formed." It is for this reason that the shamans study every issue holistically. Viewing the problem comprehensively, the behavior is assessed in terms of its strengths and weakness. Once the multifaceted roots of an issue are understood, then the shaman can lead the student into a new perspective on the problem. Doing so alters the situation entirely. The nature of the blockage determines the intervention.

Some interventions are applicable in almost any case. Others, such as medicinal or psychotropic spirits, for example, are used only when necessary. In fact, some shamanic schools go to great lengths in avoiding the use of psychotropics altogether. There is likely a time and place for both.

Healing an unhelpful habit must involve insight and feeling, both. If insight and feeling can connect with the source of the unhelpful habit, then, under the correct conditions, powerful transformation may occur. It is the shaman's role to steady this process and with the sincere attitude of the student, tremendous gains may come.

"PUT YOUR SHOULDER DOWN!"

Throughout my teenage years, those four words haunted me. I was a national skating champion, and the rigors of training involved more than 30 hours of practice each week. I worked with world class coaches who coaxed – and sometimes demanded – the best out of me.

Every skater has at least one weakness. One of mine was a stiff left shoulder. Looking back, it seems ironic. How in the world does a child develop stiffness? It's counterintuitive. We just don't associate childhood with tension. In any case, for whatever reason, a tense shoulder I had, and for the sake of our performance, it was my coach's job to find any imperfection and drill it out.

In almost every practice session, I heard the same words shouted from the pit, "Robert, put your shoulder down!" It almost became a joke. She would demand I lower my shoulder, I would insist that I did. To be honest, I never felt that it was "up" in the first place. Even watching videos of myself was of no help. I simply didn't know that anything was out of order.

Enter Tai Chi, three years later...
One night, after about a year of Tai Chi, I was doing the form, watching myself in the studio mirror. As I moved, thoughts switched back and forth between the oppressive heat and the scent of coffee, drifting up from the café on the first floor. Then, gently, softly, I noticed things slowing down. It's not easy to describe. Good Tai Chi can do this – it slows things down so you can better feel the

connection between your thoughts and their impact on your body. That night, in a moment, when thought and feeling made sense, a question whispered, surfacing in my mind. I only *just* heard it. I *almost* missed it. Looking at the guy in the mirror, I asked, "Why is his shoulder up?" In that moment, I had caught sight of someone I had never seen so fully before – myself.

In a flash, I saw myself *and* my raised left shoulder. It wasn't obvious, but it was there – certainly raised enough to crimp the picturesque lines of a skating pair. *This* is what my coach had been talking about so many years ago! I nearly burst out in a roar of laughter. I finally got it! I finally *felt* my stiff left shoulder! From the other side of the mirror, Matthew, my teacher, raised an eyebrow, peering curiously in the mirror. After class, I told him the whole story. I was elated, and he was much more serious than I expected. After a deep breath, Matthew said something I'll never forget. Few things have taught me more than what he said that night.

"Robert, it's great that you lowered your shoulder. But what does that mean?" Still bubbling with mirth, I failed to follow. I shrugged my newly freed shoulder and smiled. "I dunno," I muttered, with all the hubris of a 21-year old.

Somberly, he said, "You missed something that everyone around you could see. Those people cared about you and your benefit. They even had *proof* of where you were going wrong, but you *still* couldn't see it. Were you stubborn or numb? You even looked at it in video, and *still* couldn't see yourself. *Why?* Your mind and your body were numb to each other, at least to some degree. Because of it, you took on needless difficulty. Life's too short, kid. We can't allow a gap between mind and body. If we do, we'll miss out on things that might be the difference – *not just* between first and second place in skating, but between happiness and suffering."

Finally, I *really* got it.

SHAMANISM AND MENTAL ILLNESS

"*L*isten Doc, I know I'm not a mouse, but do the cats know it too?"

Years ago, I spoke with a psychiatrist about the shamanic. Classically trained, he believed that the shamans were individuals who, if possessing any extraordinary gifts at all, were unfortunate enough to have those gifts clouded by bi-polar if not schizoid-type personality traits.

Despite the proof of my own sanity, I have always wondered if there was any research addressing whether or not "shamanic" peoples were more or less sane than the rest of us. Considering that shamans have been pivotal social pillars since the dawn of time, the thought is compelling. In recent human history, those who may have been the shamans of the past, have been branded with every form of derision. All too often, those who hoard power feel threatened by the fluid applications of the shaman's ethical core. Western shamans have enjoyed even less tolerance than those of their global cadre.

Galileo was considered a demon-possessed heretic. Hildegard von Bingen was both loved and hated by the aristocracy who employed her skills. Saint Martin De Porres was often chided by Church elders to stop his annoying habit of appearing in multiple places at the same time. At one point, he was imprisoned to thwart his movement, but he still used his skills to visit the faithful, in parts far removed! The truth is, those in power have often found the shamans as much trouble as they are worth. In times of disfavor, the path of least resistance is to label the shamans as insane and dangerous. Ironically, as the research shows, not only is a true shaman a sane man or woman, they are perhaps the least dangerous person in society.

According to the research, shamanistic individuals are not only not insane, but may be much healthier than the rest of us. As part of the vision quest, the shaman must come to terms and harmonize the "shadow self," those parts of our personality we find unhelpful in the pursuit of standardized goals. The shamans are the men and women who are absolutely sane but creative enough to administer advice, cures and interventions, seeking the fullest benefit and harmony with the natural cycles on which we depend. Greed, hatred, and animosity cannot thrive in a shaman's heart. If they did, the results of their work would be poisoned arrows returning to the sender at the appropriate time. The law of karma is inescapable.

Having harmonized themselves, the shamans see the universal inner workings clearly. "No one wins when anyone loses," is their motto. Their gifts benefit all, with no strings attached. For that reason, those who wish to hoard power disdain the shaman – but still come to them when in need of help. The shaman is only insane when viewed from the neurotic point of view. And so, if you are ready to explore the fullness of yourself, then fear not the shaman's path. Find a path which is in harmony with life, and walk. Simply walk in balance, be in balance, and enjoy balance, and so many of the details will take care of themselves on their own.

AN AMERICAN SHAMAN
The Botanist, *Luther Burbank*

A New Englander, born in 1849, Luther Burbank enjoyed the glory of the four Northeastern seasons. As a child, he was fascinated by the natural world. The young Burbank spent hours among the flowers, the fields, and the animals that roamed between them, ever wondering about the powerful forces that shape and influence life. Botany became his way to express his unique gifts for the benefit of mankind.

Luther Burbank was well known for what many considered odd behavior. Primary among those odd behaviors was his penchant for talking with the plants under his care. Though every good gardener knows the benefit of such conversations, many were not convinced. In time, Burbank would be vindicated.

Today, many of the plants we use as food stock come directly from the genealogies established by Burbank nearly 100 years ago. A review of the species attributed to Burbank dazzles the mind. How did one man achieve such a seamless partnership with nature? How is it that one man, before the advent of powerful genetic manipulation, was able to create and maintain one stellar crop producer after another? According to him, it was in the application of direct communication with the plant itself. Burbank's success was based on relating with the living truth of the plant. It sounds strange at first, but keep reading. The proof of it is all throughout this book – and all throughout life.

One of Burbank's most famous achievements was the development his thornless roses. What's even more astonishing is that he achieved this result in a botanical blink of an eye. Usually, plant adaptations take many generations to develop. Not for Burbank! Burbank was able to breed roses without thorns in one generation, which is virtually unheard of. Aware that Burbank did not use genetic manipulation, a friend of the scientist asked how he achieved such remarkable results. Burbank replied, "It's because I talk to them. I tell them they are safe, and they do not need their thorns."

Burbank died in 1926, and enjoyed incredible prominence and respect during his life. He was well known to politicians and people of distinction. Food science is indebted to his work. All of those things are well known. Strangely, it is little known that Luther Burbank was also well acquainted with one of the last century's pre-eminent shamans, Paramahansa Yogananda. We should not be surprised that the likes of these saintly men found one another. In time, we shall explore those connections more deeply. For now, let us close with a quotation from Burbank, and the knowledge that our world is much better for having witnessed him.

"The fact is that you cannot see all of the facts about anything just by looking at the thing itself. To learn part of the essential truth about grasses for instance, you have to study the cow! A fact is relative, and if it is placed out of its relative position, it apparently is not a fact, often." - Luther Burbank

PALO SANTO

*P*alo means "stick;" *san to* means "saint" or "holy." Palo Santo therefore means a "holy stick." "What makes a stick holy?" the young girl asked. Her Padrino smiled and gave her a pat on the head.

In every single shamanic tradition, there is the belief that natural elements carry a power unique to themselves. This power is a fraction of the universal potential. Each natural element has a power, a vibration of effect. That is to say, the vibration held within a rose, the ability of a rose to evoke a response from nature, is entirely different than the vibration held within a steel column. For about the last 300 years, the concept that matter held a vibration, let alone consciousness, was viewed as heresy by the standard scientific community.

Fortunately, in the last 50 years, science is remembering the fundamentals it forgot. Science is realizing that it must rewrite many of the presumptions born from the so-called "Scientific Revolution." Although the scientific revolution certainly turned things upside down, I prefer to call it the "Scientific Resolution." During that time, a few people decided what would and what would not be a valid part of scientific experience. Some of their discoveries have been helpful, but some should be reinvestigated. Here is a brief synopsis of how the West lost its shamanic roots.

About 400 years ago, the scientific community resolutely decided to form an image of the world according to a very narrow band of presumptions, some of them incorrect. That community discarded much of the native wisdom that had fed life since antiquity.

The result was a wide-scale loss of information that was deemed heresy, superstition, and myth. Fortunately for us, with the dawn of quantum mechanics, psychoneuroimmunology, and increased precision of measurement, we are beginning to see that not only is the world stranger than we imagine, it is stranger than we CAN imagine.

"Nina, when God's energy moves through creation, little bits come here and there to serve a purpose. When the energy comes into human life, it becomes a person. And, as people, we have a great chance to mold and shape our lives. But, when God's energy goes into a flower, or an herb, it can help people, animals and the world in some way. *Palo Santo* serves creation with many, many functions. I will teach them to you. My child, when I was young, my grandmother told me that when a man or a woman lives does many good things, that person is called a saint. Some saints even seem to have magical powers. Well, Nina, this stick has a very good heart, and it can do many good things. For that reason, we call it *Palo Santo*."

THE FLOATING LAMA

One day, in 2008, I had the opportunity to speak with a long-time student of a much respected Tibetan lama. In conversation, my fellow student pulled me close and voiced in whispered tones, "Robert, you are not going to believe what one of the junior lamas told me. I'm not going to tell you who told me, but it concerns the visiting teacher." Without delay, I answered, "I'm game, what'd he say?"

His voice sounded of utter amazement. I had never seen this practical, professionally accomplished man so utterly astounded in all the years I had known him. I waited with bated breath for him to begin. I didn't have to wait long.

"A few weeks ago, a junior lama who I have known for years and whose reputation is beyond reproach, told me about an event that happened one night as he went to make prayers in the shrine room." Impatiently, my fellow student then broke his story to be certain I knew the context. "You know who I'm talking about, right? – the visiting lama.

"Of course. I've attended a few of his classes," I said. Still overtaken by amazement, he continued. "One night, while the junior lama was rounding the corner into the shrine room, he noticed something that made him stop in his tracks. Looking through the glass door into the shrine room, the junior lama saw the master in full lotus meditation posture, floating above the floor." Stunned, the junior lama took his hand off the door knob and slowly, quietly

made his way downstairs. "I don't know how many people he has told, and I don't know why I'm telling you, but, what do you think about that, Robert?"

Rhetorical question I suppose. Is "wow" an understatement?

Actually, levitation among the Tibetan masters is so common an occurrence as to be considered mundane. In fact, few would raise an eyebrow if even a devotee reported levitation. For those who walk freely in the miraculous, such events are mere evidence of often un-tapped universal potential, nothing to get excited about in and of itself. The real issue is, despite special skills, does the practitioner fol-low Dharma well? According to my sources, if the cost of achieving special skills is a decrease in the quality of your practice, the cost is too great. "Many people get stuck in realms, attached to occult func-tions," said one practitioner who wished to remain nameless. "Let such things happen of their own accord; place all your attention on the simple straightforward application of Dharma."

The human body is possessed of tremendous powers left untapped by most. These powers can be activated by holistic development or obsessive pursuit. The only difference is the resulting karmas they create. One teacher said to me, "Robert, extraordinary powers (*referred to as "siddhi" in Sanskrit*) do not necessarily indicate refinement." In fact, it's just like "The Force" in Star Wars. Whether it is levitation or something else, when a realized master manifests a power, then, even when it is done with, he or she is still a good person. On the other hand, when the obsessive egomaniac is no longer able to maintain the force of will required to sustain his powers, he is still as greedy, partial, and fearful as ever. Not only do his displays create difficulty now, they provide a tremendous barrier to the soul after death.

MIND GATE SELF STUDY
The Method of the Sun

The method of the sun uses a concept, a specific thought to promote balance. The concept is simple, but the results bear tremendous fruit the more we use it.

Method of the Sun - Reflection

As the saying goes, "The sun rises slowly, but even a blind man
knows it's hot." The sun shines on everything in equal measure.
Similarly, the fundamental realities of life are truly indisputable. If
people base their life on the indisputable wisdom of nature, then
stress will be relieved, tensions will be smoothed away, and natural
power will grow. On the other hand, if people try to act like the sun,
try to place other beings beneath them, then their own body will be
consumed by the heat they pretend to possess. The heat of imbalance is often expressed as excess ambition. This "heat" manifests as
irritability in the first stage and numb abandon later on. Fortunately,
no matter where we find ourselves, there is always a way back to
balance.

Social Solutions

In every situation, try to see the common ground and release
stubborn attachment to things that are not universal. The methods
of the sun involve recognizing life, death, love, learning, and all the
forces that control human life. The fundamentals are the essentials
of life. According to the masters, anything beyond the essence should

be handled carefully. Often, we ignore the fundamentals because we want something so badly. At other times, we try to take a shortcut. That is usually the sign of an ego out of balance.

The next time you find yourself at odds with someone, try to build upon the similarity of what is fundamental, and aligned with the natural way. And be gentle. Find what is indisputable, and co-operate with that. The more practice you get, the better the result, and no one will "lose." On the spiritual path, you will sometimes encounter energies you cannot resist. Understanding the nature of power – and how to harmonize with power – will be invaluable. Harmonizing does not mean insisting upon your agenda, but nei-ther does it mean abandoning common sense to avoid confronta-tion. The method of the sun is about true strength and true humil-ity. Taken together, we will find solutions that work for everyone involved.

Occasionally, you will find times when the path of the sun is not optimal. In those cases, the way of the Moon may be your guide.

THE PULSE

Explosions, one by one. I couldn't believe it. One by one, my organs appeared to be shaking as the master directed his energy towards them to assess their health. I had only felt something similar to this two times before. This time, nearby a local theater in Woodstock New York, one of my teachers agreed to perform a specialized assessment of me. Beneath the intermittent light of a security lamp, we began. He began with the heart.

"Heart, good," the Master said. Then he went on to the rest of the central organs, in sequence. Through pursed lips and with a vise-like grip on my inner wrist, he continued. "Lungs, good" he said, and then liver, and stomach and the spleen. He ended with my kidneys. "Kidneys, . . not bad. No disease, but you should give them a rest." It would be a few weeks before I learned what the master meant by that.

I spent a long time studying with this teacher. He is somewhat controversial. Although he bears responsibility for much of this, the man has serious skill. I have been on the receiving end of his "bridge hands," and have received premonitions from him. Beyond that, as described above, I have personally witnessed incredible feats of energetic skill. There is much complexity to this man, and there is much to learn. Although some say he is not an easy teacher to learn from, his skills are among the best I've seen.

TONGUE MAGIC

*T*he tongue is a powerful symbol of the spiritual and the sexual. In spiritual rapture, the tongue falls silent, and yet the tongue sets the tone for romantic interludes. Both speech and the finer points of physical stimulation rely on the tongue. Gaining skill with the tongue is of great importance in matters, spiritual and sexual. In keeping with its obvious importance, the tongue holds a special place in the shamanic practices of ancient Asia.

According to the Vedic and Chinese traditions, the tongue supports strength and vigor of a number of important energy meridians and glands. Within both traditions there are methods taught to increase the length, strength, and range of the tongue. Within both traditions, using the tongue can unlock important skills and draw you nearer to your beloved.

Fundamental Exercise for Strengthening the Tongue and Associated Glands
One of the most beneficial exercises for the tongue comes from the Chinese tradition. This exercise will strengthen the heart, and tone the glands and meridians encircling the mouth and throat. The teeth and gums are also helped by this. Start off with only 9 to 18 repetitions. Use this simple exercise as a part of your warm ups. Once you can manage that, proceed to doing 36 repetitions at a time. Once you reach skill with 36 repetitions, you may increase the number of repetitions so that at one sitting you are practicing,

36, 72 or 108 repetitions accordingly. Practice the skill for 30 days and then take a break for a while. After a few months, take up the practice again incorporating the set into your warm ups. Once you achieve the fundamental skill, you can return to the practice periodically to bone up on performance.

Place the tip of your tongue on the midline on the outside of your two front teeth. Then, begin to circle your tongue clockwise around the exterior of your upper teeth. Circle the tongue to the right, and then, when you reach your last upper right side tooth (upper right molar), let your tongue fall to the outside of your lower right back teeth (lower right molar). Proceed to move your tongue across the bottom row of teeth, all the way around until you reach the back bottom left tooth (lower left molar). Now, slide your tongue up to the left upper back tooth (upper left molar) and begin to run the tongue along the upper left teeth until you complete the circle and wind up back at the midline between your two front teeth.

Complete your repetitions, and then switch directions. Once you have completed the circle from right to left, and then do another set moving your tongue from the midline in the other direction. If you like, you can also run your tongue on the inner surface of the teeth. The same directions apply, just do it on the inside of the teeth as opposed to the outside.

Regular practice of this method will strengthen the heart, the mouth and the glands of the head and neck. Although a dexterous tongue will be invaluable for love, the benefits of this simple technique reach far beyond the bedroom. Don't neglect this technique and revisit it often. With correct practice, you'll be glad you did.

GIVING BIRTH

*F*rancisco shouted wildly, throwing his arms into the air, "Magic and miracles are everywhere man, we just gotta be open to 'em". Leaning back in that rickety chair, looking into the sky, he told the kind of story I would hear frequently in the years to come. The August night seemed to pause in anticipation.

"She came to us full of hope. She wanted her baby to be healthy, and she wanted to be healthy too. Our reading said the baby had a good chance the cord would be wrapped around its neck. Sometimes this is very dangerous. We had to avoid that or make sure nothing bad happened. Doctors say that most times there is nothing you can do, but not in this case. Stroking his modest goatee, Francisco continued.

His fingers tapping the table between us, he said, "It could have turned out badly. Sometimes it does." Then, with a sweeping gesture of his palm, he continued. "We asked Orisha what we should do, and did what we could. Then, we let go and let life do the rest. That's how it's done in our tradition. Do you get it? People feel at peace, doing their best and working in harmony with the principle of life. You can't take a shortcut. Shortcut life and it will often shortcut you."

Francisco leaned forward and put more leaves into the iron pot. The sunset shone on his face, golden, like the embers burning inside that small cauldron. Inside the pot, glowing charcoal bent and burned whatever touched it. Snapping and bending the leaves, an aroma of power and intrigue emerged. Somehow, it seemed the smoke wanted to speak. As if on cue, a warm breeze wafted the smoke in front of us. Taking a deep breath, Francisco finished his tale. Although tests did confirm that the cord was wrapped around his neck, the child was born without without ill effect. Score one for the shamans.

What Francisco said resonated deep inside me, especially the idea of asking spirit for guidance and then feeling at peace with doing your best. According to the master shamans, feeling at peace with your best efforts, doing good work, and then, having faith in grace, are the foundations. If you can get that – really get it – then the rest usually falls into place. Navigating the intersection of faith and works is the master key of high-quality shamanism. Misunderstanding the interplay of faith and efforts is the spiritual pitfall of many. "This should be studied carefully," a priest once advised.

SEXUAL INITIATION
AND FAMILY STRUCTURE

Sex is happening all the time. I don't mean just at the physical level. Sex is the interplay of substantial and insubstantial, the dance of form and function. It is the force of generations and it is our lineage. At the same time, sex is the body, mind, and soul of ecstasy.

Approaches to sexuality in shamanism are quite varied. Some schools advocate celibacy, others, rank hedonism. The presence of both extremes likely indicates a balance point somewhere in the middle. At the very least, we can say there is a balance point informed by circumstance.

I came across a story of a Latin American shaman who described how sexuality is taught in his tribe. Not uncommon is the "taking" of a young man by a much more experienced woman. The initiatory relationship is not usually an emotional one, nor is it usually a commitment. In fact, it seems merely to be a release valve for lustful curiosity. The tribe permits the relationship so that the young man has an idea of what he ought to do when he's married later on. There may be some merit to the theory, under the conditions, but it doesn't always work out well.

Every now and then an older adult gets too deeply involved with a young adult. In such cases, when the unaware spouse finds out, the young lover may find his or her life in jeopardy! Such is the cost of inappropriate relations. None the less, it is the code of the tribe that if a family is destabilized by wanton sexuality, the affront is corrected. One or two examples of such "correction" are enough to make sure that extramarital affairs are the exception not the rule.

These days, we flaunt a casual sexuality. There are far-reaching implications of this. On an individual level, confusion arises when there is little or no social consequence for inappropriate sexuality. There is a distinction between education and error. For the shaman, an unwanted pregnancy might be a social catastrophe. Affairs might cause intertribal war or destruction of the tribe itself. And so, regardless of liberal initiatory practices, the family unit was seen as sacred and an object worthy of tremendous respect. Perhaps more than we do now, tribal people know the value of a family unit. In our modern society, where there are proxies for nearly every station in life, we seem to think that family isn't much more than a reference point. Nothing could be farther from the truth. Family is your connection to the ancestors; family is your blood and your connection to the land. Neglecting family and endangering the sexuality which builds those families is a woeful mistake indeed.

CREATION

In the fall of 2009, I found myself once again near a small pond deep in the Northeastern woods. Fall had not yet come, but the leaves of the sugar maple had already begun to show veins of red and gold among the dominant greenery enclosing them. The air was still humid, but not oppressively so. As I navigated the shoreline, I stopped to check in on a favorite friend, goldenrod.

Goldenrod is a powerful medicine. And its personality is just as strong, although demure. Often, when I am working with goldenrod, flashes happen, sparks of awareness not unlike the brilliant gold that explodes from the reserved composure of its stem and leaves. This day, as I crouched in the brush, listening to its messages, something wonderful happened. Just as I ducked into the undergrowth, only a few hairs above the cover, I heard wings in the air. I was not the only one about to take a rest.

Looking left, I saw the majestic blue heron begin its descent onto the shoreline. Even more amazingly, it was coming straight at us!

No sooner did this thought register in my mind than did the heron become aware I was there. I'm sure I flashed just like the goldenrod. Swiftly, the heron drew up its center and begin to bank in, towards the midpoint of the pond, only to leave the scene – as surprised as I was, I'm sure.

The moment of its approach changed time. Three worlds had come together. In the moment of transition, we were all surprised, and as it turned, its wings came very close to the water, and I saw this, and those wings, without touching the water, stirred the surface into concentric ribbons of life. I remember everything about that moment. The sun, the wind, dappled patterns shifting on the water's surface. I remember the scents and the sounds around me. Meaning is deeper than information. All of this encoded in three simple lines.

Waterfowl
Your feathers brush the water
Circle upon circle begins

We must take care of Mother Nature, for she is the deepest most fulfilling parts of ourselves. As we devastate her through egotistical engineering, we destroy ourselves, brick by brick, cell by cell.

INTERSECTIONS AND
THE GARDEN OF MIND

*T*he mind is like a garden. The quality of what grows there will impact your experience and the quality of your life. Life is an intersection, an interaction between what you hold, unaware, what you think you know you have, and the myriad of conditions arising from without. There are so many challenges, it is good to be able to balance the ones we can manage.

Joan Borysenko, Deepak Chopra, Einstein and even Schrodinger have all confirmed that the state of our minds not only affects the quality of the human body, but also impacts the development of the universe itself. Such luminaries are not alone in their discovery of these truths. The shamans knew this long before words took form. Importantly, however, just as you are co-creating the reality of your body, mind and universe, so too are others. As a result, although you are the prime author in the experience of your life, others are co-creating along with you. There are moments of intersection.

Each thought you have, every action you perform, sends waves of reality into the quantum ocean that is existence. The various waveforms we create interact with the waveforms of others. The result is a consensus reality. It is not that we all agree upon what we think is reality, reality congeals by default. Tyranny of the majority is one possibility; so too is the tyranny of a few who use trickery and anger, luring the unwitting into the predictable death of spirit.

After taking shape, consensus reality then loops back into your heart and mind. The feedback loop either encourages or discourages balance and happiness. For this reason, the shamans guard the ocean of mind zealously. Do not carelessly let thoughts enter your mind. Do not mindlessly involve yourself in trash. Ensure that what you believe is not only in harmony with the process of life on which you depend, but in fact, also benefits as many beings as possible, in as many ways as possible, without hindering the actualization of full potential in harmony with life.

Tend the garden of your mind responsibly. Compassionately engage the minds of others. If you want your children to inherit a world of peace, begin to live peace now. Watch the waves go out, and observe what returns. For a while though, you'll have to deal with the pollution you may have sent out before you recognized the power of thought. Be patient, be hopeful, have faith in the process; the proof is all around.

Just as scientists confirm the creative process of existence, all spiritual masters agree that once old negative thoughts are exhausted and the effects of negativity are spent, balance and harmony will return. It's only a matter of time.

"Take hold the reigns of the heart, never let the horses of mind run unattended."   - Zen proverb.

MIND GATE SELF STUDY
The Method of the Moon

*A*ll life is interconnected. Because of this connection, we can emulate the principles of nature underlying all existence. Just as the moon borrows all its brilliance from the sun, the moon exhibits the darkness of space when stillness is required. The applications of the Method of the Moon are manifold.

Method of the Moon
Correct Following

Imagine that you're arguing with a person who is being very difficult. Perhaps he stubbornly holds a view that will bring difficulty to everyone involved. In that moment, that stubborn individual is attempting to dominate the situation by embodying the power of the sun. If he hangs on too long, he will burn out because, although believing himself to be great like the sun, he is at best a light bulb. Of course, such a person doesn't know that. You, on the other hand, know better. As a result, you wait patiently, allowing his or her energy to be spent. When the time is right, when the power of ego fades, join in with that person, affirm the good, and offer your perspective on how his and your ideas may merge in the direction of peace. Repeating this cycle as many times as needed, the vast feeling of peace you represent will eventually and naturally draw the person to reconsider things in light of harmony and health. There are of course, exceptions.

"Thrashing about in the river, he only got cut. His blood stained the river; he didn't remember how to follow the power of the water. If he followed the water, he would have been protected. He came back next year with more scars, but he finally made it through. All young medicine men must learn to harmonize with powers stronger than the self." — **Native American Elder**

A GERMAN MYSTIC
Hildegard von Bingen

A controversial figure in her own time, Von Bingen stirs controversy even today. Born in the 11th Century, she was an enigma for many who knew her. Some believed she was saintly, others thought she was crazy. There is evidence enough to keep the argument going. Perhaps only the eyes of the mystic can reach any certain conclusion. What is known is that despite the complexity of her character, Von Bingen was a mystic, and some would say a Christian shaman. Whatever you believe her to be, there is profound meaning embedded in her work.

Visions struck the young girl in her youth. Throughout her childhood, she was prone to bouts of intense concentration and adoration of God's work in nature. Von Bingen would often be found roaming the forests, "talking" with plants and even minerals. Von Bingen was convinced that God was instructing her on the medicinal uses of these elements. She inspired many, but her example may have been uncomfortable for others. Having been born to a royal family, few believed she comported herself as nobility should. Perhaps for this reason, the young Von Bingen was dedicated to the local convent. Quickly, the odd behaviors which made her a curiosity in the secular world brought her tremendous renown in the world of medieval Christianity.

> *"At the time of man's creation, all the elements of the Earth were subject to him. Because they knew that he was alive, they worked*

with him in all his actions, and he worked with them. And the Earth sprouted greenness in accordance with his race, nature, customs and ways of humans. For the Earth has many herbs that reach out to peoples spiritual needs, and yet they are distinct from people... Nevertheless, certain of these herbs can cure the noxious and unhealthy moistures in people with the art of healing."

- Hildegard Von Bingen, *Physica*

Von Bingen's "art of healing" made use of medical knowledge that had come down to her not only by divine revelation but also through a well preserved tradition of herbal medicine. That tradition had flourished in the Rhine valley since antiquity. All indigenous people have their medical traditions, and those traditions make use of the ecological community in which they arise. Von Bingen's idea that the Earth sprouts herbs in accordance to man's spiritual needs is compelling in light of this. Luther Burbank confirms this and preempts modern biochemistry discussing how plants do indeed change their biochemistries quite dynamically. Plants talk to other plants and in fact "interpret" environmental cues as either favorable or unfavorable for growth. Just as a child may fail to thrive in an emotionally vacant household, so too may plants be accorded all the raw materials, but fail to reach potential, owing to many subtle causes.

Von Bingen was a trailblazer. In a time when women were often disrespected, she became a consultant to popes, nobility, and a hero to the sick in need of help. She was a master herbalist, composer, writer, and much more. Her life offers up amazing inspiration and we will draw on that inspiration in our journey.

EMULATING NATURE

*E*verything has its time and season. This timing comes from the way that life and its interconnections seek harmony. Yes, life is seeking harmony. Can you believe it?

For people, harmony arrives in honoring the cycles of life. The cycles of life are the inner structure of the universe touching all things, even you and me. "Finding *your* path is the way of building your happiness *and* letting others do the same." So said a physician and Medicine Man of the Alaskan Inuit.

There is a time to shine and a time to let others shine. There is a time for action, and a time for deep rest. All things follow this way. "This is the dharma (code) of human life," said Master Liu. Continuing, she warned, "If people don't follow it, they create trouble in this life, and it will follow them after death. Karma can never be cheated; people should choose carefully. Not that life has no compassion, but sometimes we choose to learn the hard way. It's better to choose wisely, seeing that everything is connected."

Human life comes from nature, and intelligence guides the universe. Science now confirms this is true. Too bad it took science so long to catch up with our native wisdom!

If humanity declares itself intelligent, then intelligence has to come from somewhere. Intelligence is either inherent in existence, or bestowed at a certain time. The footprints of intelligence are everywhere. If humanity declares its own intelligence, then it must concede the roots of intelligence! "You can't have your cake and eat it too."

Intelligence is the very substance of existence, despite our ability to believe it isn't so. In fact, to someone at peace with this perspective, evidence of the Creator, the ground luminosity, the Grandfather of the Native Americans is undeniable. To someone living in dualistic illusion, under the strain of maintaining its barriers apart from the rest of existence, there will be no proof to satisfy the reality of Spirit. Those who have deep-seated fear and ego fragmentation must come to terms with the intimacy of life to know the reality of God and life's purpose. Intimacy is not sexual agitation. Intimacy is the baby in the womb of its mother, or the quiet passion attesting to the depth of your soul mate's love. Those who will not be gentle and look at themselves deeply will never know the full flowering of the grace available right here and right now.

The intelligence within humanity links us to the intelligence imbuing all existence, in all its forms. Relating to the ubiquity of this intelligence is the essence of shamanism. Aware of this connection, we may cooperate with nature's power. Because of this connection, we can emulate the principles of nature underlying all existence. So much of our native wisdom comes from understanding and accepting this tremendous gift of the Creator operating in our lives.

REVIVING A DEAD FISH

In the fall of 2005, I attended a training intensive with the Shi family of Danbury, Connecticut. The Shi's Chinese Healing Arts Center has been a landmark of natural healing for nearly 20 years. All comers have walked through their doors, and nearly every patient I've met has shared with me a personal story of healing. On this day however, my friend and I would witness a special kind of healing we never expected.

After a long day of classes, Dr. Huang entered the classroom and called out the younger students. "You young students, you can use your youth to catch fish and help us move the fish from the shallow pool to the deep one. But you have to be quick, we don't want the fish to feel stress."

My classmate and I humorously rolled our eyes. It always seemed that whenever we made the trek to Danbury, either Dr. Huang or her husband, Master Shi, always found some odd task for us to do. "I guess it's kind of like washing the floors at the dojo," my buddy said. With a laugh I countered, "Yeah, this must be the Chinese Medicine version, I suppose. Fish scooping."

With cups and nets in hand, my compatriot and I arrived at edge the large water fountain in front of the center. Like good fishermen, we strategically arranged the pools rocks in such a way that the fish would be corralled into a *cul de sac* near the center of the pool. The scene was a fiasco! Despite the fact that we had arranged everything in our favor, these fish were tough to catch. They jumped, wiggled and darted so quickly that we weren't sure we'd beat the setting sun. And then, from a second floor window, a voice, "Boys, it's getting cold these days. You have to finish before tonight or the fish will die when the water gets cold. Stop playing around and catch them." It may have looked like we were playing around, but let me tell you, this was hard work!

In our renewed zeal to catch the fish, one rather large-sized fish caught my eye, and I thought I could catch it. Unfortunately, I was wrong. Jabbing quickly with my net, I had cornered the fish and was about to scoop it up, when it made an unexpected last ditch effort at evasion. Reacting to this move, I jammed my net into the crevice from which the fish sprang. I felt something collapse. I withdrew my net immediately. A few feeble twists and turns and then the fish just floated to the surface, just in time to embarrass me. As Dr. Huang stepped onto the porch, my buddy screamed, "You killed it! You killed the fish!" I shot him a look that could burn steel. Mortified, I addressed Dr. Huang, "I'm sorry Dr. Huang. He zigged when he should have zagged." With a look of impatience, she said, "You have to be more careful, they are delicate. Where is it?"

"Over there," I mumbled.

It had been about a minute since I crushed it. Bending down, cradling the fish out of the water, Dr. Huang said a few words, enclosed the fish in her palms as she walked to the deep pool in the back. I don't know how or why, but when she put that fish back in the water, it darted away as if nothing had happened. "Sometimes they just need a push, Robert. Chi Power." she said with a smile. With that she strolled inside, and my classmate and I looked at each other completely amazed.

RELATING TO TIME

"Time wasn't really running out," said a Taino Shaman. "But still, the Mayans had to finish their work, and time was the major factor. But for them, time was not the same as we think it is." For the ancients of the American peninsula, time was very close to God. Those who understood time were close to God. And for those who misused the gift of time, troubles would come.

Timekeepers are sometimes shamans, but shamans are most often beyond time. The very nature of shamanism indicates the plasticity of time. Time can be changed. Time is not a constant. Quantum physics affirms the same. Amazing how so called primitive people were ahead of Quantum Physics by more than 5,000 years! In fact, so-called "primitive thought" unlocks many of the mysteries on the meaning and purpose of life.

In recent years, scientists have clearly shown that not only is time not constant, time is plastic. Time is changeable, depending on conditions. Physicist Gary Zukav cites numerous examples showing that the qualitative framework of an observer affects time, not only in the subjective sense, but in what we usually call the objective as well. Reworded in shaman-speak, we dream the universe we live.

Not everyone dreams the same dream. As a result, if we wish to experience large-scale, population-sized shifts of time, then large-scale numbers of observers need to comply. There are factors affecting compliance – that's another story. Though we don't typically recognize it, one of the largest mass complicities of history is the way that "civilized" societies have bought into, (literally "bought into") a shared concept of time. Buying time is a side effect of civilization in need of balance.

"Who did the civilizing," a shaman asks. He follows with the rhetorical answer: "Someone who had something to gain by rendering time into a commodity. Someone who had something to gain from reinforcing an illusion of fragmentation. White and dark skinned people both did this," he adds. It makes me think. Who began the chain of civilization? Who civilized *them*? Here's a hint: It isn't the English, the Egyptians, or any other society. It's deeper and more fundamental. Civilization as a code of conduct has benefits, but those changes must not come at the expense of wholeness.

According to the shamans, what we have purchased with time is not always equal to what we have lost. Time is a tool, nothing more. "We are on par with time, for we all emerge from the nature of being," said one practitioner. Time is measured by the subject, not the other way around. The "original" people of each culture knew how to work with time. Not many of "the Originals" who remain have been able to flourish in a world gone mad with our modern view of time. This is not to say that time is inherently bad. However, just like any other tool, we lose something in ourselves when we do not relate to a thing correctly. Correcting our relationship with time is one benediction offered by the authentic shamanic traditions.

CATCHING THE MIND

Raindrops falling,
A misshapen leaf
In the form of a toad
I stop in mid stride

MIND GATE SELF STUDY
Cadence, Rhythms and Time

*P*eople are thinking and feeling beings. Thought and feeling are rhythmic and follow the ebb and flow of events. When our thoughts and feelings fall into step with rhythmic signals, the result is called entrainment. This is a cosmic phenomenon. Planets are entrained in their orbits, atoms by the subatomic heartbeats of the quantum world. Lovers are entrained by one another.

Entrainment is based upon the rhythm of perception. One of the unique – and often overlooked – qualities of human life is that we can adjust our rate of perception based on conditions. That is to say, a rhythm that might entrain others need not do so for us all.

Entrainment has been a shamanic tool since the earliest times. The Shaman approaches it with choice, and the quality of the resulting state is evaluated by its impact on holistic full potential. Traditionally, dance and music entrain cultural unity and dynamism. But entrainment can do more. Shamanic entrainment may be used to access altered states of consciousness. There are many ways to achieve altered states. Dance and music are well known methods, but more esoteric methods exist as well.

Some Shamans make use of mind-altering drugs to achieve this end. The value of a specific approach depends upon conditions. Drug induced entrainment is not universally applicable nor is it advised by most of my teachers. Nonetheless, it does have its place and time. Generally speaking, the Shaman seeks entrainment with rhythms that are in step with a holistic experience of life. Any rhythm bringing about a reduction in power, balance, and poise is evaluated and either avoided totally or handled carefully at best. The shamanic outlook is to understand entrainment to ensure that one is not lulled unaware into a rhythm which conflicts with the holistic potential of existence. The qualities of the rhythms with which we entrain powerfully impact our expression of full potential and the very quality of our lives.

Furthermore, because societies are made up of individuals, they can be entrained as well. In ancient times, tribal identity was based upon individual and group entrainment with the rhythms of one's native land. The goal of tribal living was to live life in a sustainable, holistically balanced fashion. This was expressed effortlessly as correct entrainment. Thus, understanding this principle can be a useful way to deepen our own application of this awareness. Among the Japanese Shamans, *misogi* (waterfall purification) is one such method for understanding entrainment.

About eight years ago, I was told to undergo *misogi* (waterfall cleansing), and then meditate on cadence (see below). Misogi practice is common among the Japanese shamans. Since I was heading to Japan that summer, Master Rick thought it would be a good time for me to give it a shot. Misogi involves remaining for prolonged periods of time beneath a waterfall. The process drowns out mental noise, thus allowing perception to regain fuller functioning. Such functioning is critical for making sense of life.

I did as my teacher recommended. I made the initial preparations and performed the misogi. Water crashed down around and upon me, landing with a deafening roar. Master Rick had been to this place as well, but decades earlier. He wasn't sure if I'd be able to find this place; after all, it was only my third trip to Japan, and my Japanese wasn't that good. Despite my broken Japanese, I did find it, and it made the time underneath the waterfall slightly more bearable because of my triumph. It's not easy to sit under a waterfall for an hour, but the results can be worth it. Once finished, I was clear and sharp. I moved to a quiet place, sat facing the waterfall and began my work with cadence.

Cadence means rhythm; rhythms determine what we create or destroy. How we interact with rhythms hold great importance in how we interact with life. How many times does our child seek affirmation, but we lose the chance because we are somewhere else in space or time? How many times do we speak to others, only to realize they haven't heard a word we said? All of this comes down to rhythm. We must pay attention to the rhythms we knowingly or unknowingly follow. The ability to match our rhythm with the needs at hand expands perception, ensures the best result possible and is a key to discovering the meaning and purpose of life.

With the waterfall in front of me, I watched the wall of water renew itself as quickly as it dashed upon the rocks. Experimenting with my rate of perception, it fell faster or slower depending on what I selected to view. From afar, the water seemed like a smooth sheet of glass. Closer, I found a ribbon of water turning without end. Closer still, I saw threads of water streaming down and snaking around the rocks below. Finally, I saw individual droplets, suspended as if frozen in time. Each day, we are brought into rhythm by a number of signals. The alarm clocks, traffic lights and class bells define how fast we are scheduled to move between points A and B. Rhythms are necessary, but the rhythms of one moment are not necessarily the ones best suited to another place in time and space. Carefully observe the rhythms you follow. Are they really promoting your health and full potential? Do they support the best in everyone? Do not overlook the usefulness of this method.

REVELATION AND
THE PARLOR OF MIRACLES

*T*here will come a time when you arrive at a very deep understanding of the meaning and purpose of life. Until that time,
God gives us flashes of wholeness to the degree that we may understand them. The process cannot be rushed, but we as individuals
do choose how quickly we move along the way. Ironically, believe it
or not, if that totality of understanding were to come to you now,
your life would become unrecognizable. Timing is everything. For
that reason, God reveals himself/herself to us slowly, often in stages
as life moves on. Often, even the most developed among us are not
permitted a full revelation of the Glory of God. Think of Moses.

Moses was a great leader in the ancient Middle East. Even
though Moses was nearly perfect in the eyes of God, even Moses
was not permitted to see the "face of God." According to the story,
if Moses saw the face of God, his life as he knew it would end. Some
interpret this to mean he would die. And yet, even without seeing
the face of God, Moses was very, very close to God.

In every age, there are always a few, rare men and women
who walk very close to God. Such people are often marked with
distinction in body, mind and service. As you might expect, there
are also charlatans who parade about, imitating understanding,
parroting borrowed concepts enthralling the unaware with
mischievous deception. Whether a shaman or not, we should all be
wary of those who wish to deceive. Deceivers exist in every field of
endeavor, every walk of life, male and female, alike. Life is made

much more enjoyable when people stick to the real and – as much as possible – avoid the false. One lama taught that the best guard against charlatanism is to make sure you surround yourself with those who are honest and sincerely wish for the benefit of all.

Master Shibendu once remarked you will know liars by the ego which precedes, walks with, and remains after the miscreant has departed. Some hide this ego rapture better than others. But just as a boat leaves a wake in its path, so it is too with people. There is always evidence of fraudulent sincerity. Overindulgence in self-importance is the clarion call of deception. False humility is another. Both excessive ego attachment and false humility must be mitigated for us to draw near to God. Arrogance precedes a fall, and the meek shall inherit the Earth. In the embrace of the Divine there is no insincerity whatsoever. Only when truthfulness dwells within our hearts can we be open enough to receive the grace that God wishes for all beings to enjoy. Only then will we arrive in the parlor of the miraculous – only then shall we see the aspect of God that is appropriate for our time and place.

THE PROCESS WE ARE IN:
The Kung Fu of a Zen Master

I would have been knocked out. His fist passed right before my nose. Almost making fun of me, Master Chin asked, "Why are you studying?" As I struggled for my balance, he asked me again, "Why can't you keep your balance? It's so easy." On its return, his fist then turned into a palm flashing before my eyes. Laughing, he finished, "If you can't even figure out what's going on here, and this close to you, what can you know about anything else? You must see the process you're in!" Often, a teacher will share a moment of imbalance so that we can see how he or she handles the situation. If we are smart, we don't merely learn a single technique of balancing, but even more, a principle for addressing all imbalance. We must learn to bring full awareness to what is close. If we miss the full impact of what is close, the error will increase as we move to what is distant.

What are your reasons for reading this book? On some level, it's probably because you are looking for insight on life. And where do we hope that insight leads? Well, in a nutshell, we are all looking for peace and balance. Both are moving targets.

The genius of I-liq-ch'uan (Mind-Force Kung-Fu), Master Chin's version of shamanism, is that his art presents balance as a dynamic awareness. Balance is seen as alterable and informed by conditions. Owing to this interdependence, the student must ever assess and adjust the parameters of balance in light of conditions. The process is reminiscent of Lao Tzu's internal alchemy. "Not too much, not too little, just the right amount, at just the right time, only this will do." So goes a Confucian remark on the subject.

The quality of Master Chin's results speak to the efficacy of his system. In more than eight years of studying with the man, I not only saw no one beat him, no one even came close. At one point, near the beginning of his public career, entrenched members of the Kung Fu community labeled his arts as nothing more than a series of tricks. Tricks they are not, I can assure you. Rather, the system is one of awareness, born from a deep, organic sense of movement at its core.

If I-liq-ch'uan were nothing but tricks, then shouldn't one of the legion of challengers have been able to reveal the so-called tricks for what they were alleged to be? *No one has succeeded.* While there are some in the I-liq-ch'uan community who come close to Master Chin's skill, I myself do not. For those who seek this path to development, there are tremendous teachers and amazing things to be learned by "changing with change."

Despite the system's emphasis on change, some things never do. The core of Master Chin's Zen teachings expresses the movement between impermanence and the ever-constant, generative fountain of existence. This represents both the essence of change and the inalterable quality of foundational totality. Immersed in this apparent paradox, the I-liq-ch'uan practitioner embodies a wonderful synthesis of knowledge and application.

Profound intelligence moves in I-liq-ch'uan, and its fullness awaits those who can harmonize the ego with "suchness." Many study, few achieve. Some leave as skilled bullies, never tasting the sweetness of the art. For them, despite their abilities, the gateway to the miraculous slams shut.

HAWKING AND THE SHAMAN'S GOD

*I*n the summer of 2010, Stephen Hawking issued a proclamation declaring that because a planet similar to Earth was found orbiting a star much like our own Sun, the indication that God made life here on Earth "just to please us human beings," is highly unlikely. Hawking has since added the notion that he considers the afterlife to be a fairy tale, and that the notion of God exists only to dispel human fears of death.

With all the billing of a main event, some in the media held this revelation as the culmination of a lifetime of Hawking's study. With the anticipation that Hawking might mirror Einstein's "mind of God" statement, for many, his proclamation rang stale and a bit absurd. Others were jubilant. Still others, myself included, wondered, "What's all the fuss? Just what notion of God was Hawking addressing?" I saw nothing remarkable in his pronouncement.

Hawking seems to be saying that the notion of God rests upon the idea that human life is the only life in the universe, and if it is not, then God doesn't exist. Trouble is, I don't know anyone whose belief in God is so parochial. Even the Vatican, a stronghold of conservatism, has agreed that in accordance with the Divine wish, life may exist anywhere. This opens the door to the possibility that life is less an Earth-specific phenomena and rather, an event that speaks to the creative potential of existence.

In the case of Dr. Hawking's comments, I'm surprised to see that he is either unaware of, or has not acknowledged, information which points contrary to his opinions on God and the afterlife. Perhaps we can argue the terminology of what may be called the "spiritual", but the presence of a spiritual force is well founded. Perusal of Zukav, Borysenko and Chopra provide important preliminaries.

If one argues that there is no proof of God, then there is certainly is no proof to the contrary, and there are reasons for this. Of course, we all know that one cannot prove the non-reality of something. One can only prove what exists. Such a caveat is irrelevant with respect to the spiritual, because data on the spiritual does exist. Research from the quantum sciences (both biological and physical), show the impact of a spiritual worldview. Is Dr. Hawking not aware of this evidence?

As for his viewpoint, with no data to the contrary, and with ample evidence on the reality of the spiritual, the implications are staggering. And so, the declaration that God and the afterlife are fairy-tales, is illogical. There are proofs on the reality of the spiritual, its impact can be detected and because of this, Dr. Hawking's statements must be seen and identified as opinion. We are all entitled to opinion, but sometimes the opinions of an expert (in one field of study), do not necessarily carry relevance beyond their specific field of expertise. A related issue, is the recent press surrounding the possibility of Grand Unification Theory. Once again, our wisdom traditions may enrich discussion.

Currently, many physicists are searching for what is called the Grand Unification Theory (GUT). GUT represents a quest for a certain set of formula, envisioned as being able to predict all events that have or ever will occur. The mystery of GUT has not yet been solved. Recent evidence indicates that arriving at the nature of GUT may be impossible, without accounting for a long forgotten subjective factor - the power of choice, manifest as mind. The nature of mind, sometimes called consciousness, is profound. The powers of the mind may only be guessed at. None the less, the tremendous impact of the mind is real and has recently been recognized by a specialized type of mathematics called game theory.

Future developments will likely show that the missing link in the elusive, "Grand Unification Theory", may only be found when we recognize the meaning of consciousness itself. There is an important reason this may be so.

When conscious life, in our case, human beings, do not account for the very intelligence from which thinking takes shape, errors compound. It is imperative to accept the implications of conscious matter. In order to see comprehensively, we must accept the nature of ourselves. We are conscious matter. We are thinking matter, reflectively looking back upon ourselves. And that is perhaps, is the hardest thing to grasp.

Our global wisdom traditions suggest that if we do not come to terms with the nature of mind and matter, then all our surmising are prone to tremendous error. Life cannot make sense when it is viewed incorrectly. The tides of time bear the evidence of such confusion. The Brahma sutra beckons, "Life is not one, there are not two!"

Seeking the mysteries of existence without accounting for the ubiquity of consciousness is the proverbial dog chasing the tail of the canine he believes is following him. *And yet we persist.* It is not easy to see ourselves. Oddly, seeing ourselves comprehensively, free of bigotry - is a pre-requisite for most spiritual paths. It would be good if academics required this as well. I am reminded of the Jedi.

Oddly, the balance between objective and subjective requires effort. Effort is required because habitual conditioning (the default operation when conscious matter fixates upon its reflexive relationship to itself), tends to generate a highly localized view of events. Attachment to that localized view must be mitigated, or the impact is an unconsciousness forming a future of increasingly probable errors.

So difficult is accurate "self-seeing", that to achieve the minimum criteria of insight in many schools of Tibetan Buddhism for example, requires three years, three months and three days in retreat (depending on the school). The old seminarians of Medieval Europe lived in apprenticeship for a decade or more. Every traditional culture maintained a similar path for those who would do the work. The historical prevalence of these practices acknowledges the truth, that an operational understanding of what may be called "spiritual insight" (that is, information which meaningfully integrates mind and matter), must come at the cost of mitigating the neurotic mind-body split.

In the case of the Tibetan Buddhists, most of the retreat is spent in meditation. The three year retreat is journeyed under the tutelage of a Master practitioner. The Master practitioner exists to shed light on the many hiding places of the ego. To the degree the ego refuses to accept the implication of holistic existence, there will be errors of thought and deed. The Masters say that tremendous things insight and benefit are possible when the ego arrives at a full accounting of itself and in relationship to being.

Although, there is not only one single path to accurate self seeing, none the less, those who succeed, usually emerge with a very similar message. Although differences insight may be notices, those differences do not detract from the reality of the inspirational source. The results of the Master practitioners indicate there is value in the established, age old practices.

In the spiritual paths of which I am aware, each aspect of the self and its impact upon the perceptual field must never leave awareness. *It's a tall order.* Anything less and we fall into the habitual cycles of psycho-social conditioning (not all conditioning is healthy). When the mind abides in habitual conditioning, the subject-object split assumes prominence. In such a state of disarray, the individual ego cannot escape the gravity of a localized worldview. In many cases this holding pattern results in a stiff tension which impairs the function of body/mind.

In order to access the field of unified knowledge and benefit from the access gained, the notion of subject and object must be resolved. There is knowledge which is "the same" for all human beings. And the impact of that knowledge improves the quality and composition of one's life once it is gained. But as we have already established, effort is required, and the effort must be correct. Oddly enough, correct effort is natural, produces measurable results, while ultimately appearing effortlessness.

Grand unification requires much of us and is a lifelong process. As Confucius said, "Not too much, not too little, not too early, not too late. Just the right amount, at just the right time. Only this will do". If we would speak of truth, then all aspects of the self must be seen on a level playing field, because, all aspects of ourselves have developed in unison.

What completes the reflection is that man and God meet through the self-evident lens of reflective intelligence. Life, culminating here on Earth at this time through human existence, reflects the complete potential of life – the ground-organizing substance of existence. This can be described more generally as the ability to create and destroy, based on choice.

Beyond this, the implicit reality of God is undeniable. If there is consciousness in humanity, and humanity is made of atoms just the same as all the rest of the universe, then the universe is a mind/matter phenomena and the net sum of that may well be called God, despite our inability to grasp that reality while in the confines of human life.

Failing to recognize the implications of this fact points less to the question of the reality of God and more to our inability to come to terms with the profound nature of ourselves, and in particular, to the consciousness which is the missing link in the grand unification of it all.

REFLECTION ON SPIRITUAL REALITY
AND GRAND UNIFICATION

*C*an you imagine that your body and mind are - for all intents and purposes, stardust? Can you accept the implications that somehow and through some agency, these bits of matter express reflective thought? Mind and matter are not one, there are not two! So what then is the spiritual path? Old Kaballistic thought says we are sparks of Divine Soul and are meant to activate latent "soul-sparks" and then return to Source. It is in this way humanity interacts (by choice), with the Divine work of being. It may be an apt metaphor. The individual mind recognizes it's own nature and seeks the unified source from which its reflective self-awareness springs. Along the way, our balance may improve the balance of others. This is the prospect and the choice, and is impacted by so many variables. Perhaps we can argue the terminology associated with the Sacred, but the reality of "It", often called God and the afterlife is not at all a matter of question or fairy tale. It is in fact, the basis of reality.

SEX AND THE ROOT

Years ago, while attending my first Tai Chi classes, I remember that our teacher was fond of reminding us that "the root is in the foot." Back then, I thought he meant that physical strength and power were rooted in a good strong stance. Since I was an avid martial artist, those things were most interesting to me. It would be a while before I more fully understood the meaning of the term, "root."

"Root" is a bit like a code word in Chinese. Depending on how the word is used, root means different things. Sometimes the term can refer to the basis of skill. In another usage, it may indicate the foundation of a building or even the human body, as in the bones and structural components of the foot. Finally, "root" may also mean the raw vitality that powers our biological form. In laymen's terms, this vitality is charisma, or sexual power. Considering the many meanings of the word "root," we can discover what the ancients meant by the phrase, "the root is in the foot."

"The human body should channel power, not withhold it," said my teacher. The "channeling" is supported by balancing the physical and energetic structures of the foot. Balancing the foot balances movement – and if we are mindful, our lives, overall. Balance in movement relaxes the mind. A relaxed mind orchestrates mental and physical equilibrium more effectively. The optimal interplay of tension (notice I did not say "stiffness") and relaxation, enhances energetic flow. The results of improved energetic flow are physical and mental performance, harmonized hormonal secretions and improved charisma – i.e., raw sexual power. A roadmap on how this is done lies within the foot itself.

The "root" organs of the human body are the kidneys. The entry point of the kidney meridians are in the center of the foot. Through the kidneys, blood is purified of toxic substances that inhibit the optimal formation of vital fluids. For men, the vital fluids are contained within the sperm. For women, the vital fluids are held within the blood. According to Chinese medicine, men should be conservative in the emission of semen, and women should make sure that before and after menstruation, the blood should remain rich, thus making the regulatory work of the kidneys less stressful. "It's all about keeping the books, Bob," said Master Rick. "If you spend, you had better earn. The best way to earn is with chi (energy). One of the best ways to protect your investment is massaging the root."

An easy way for massaging the root can be done right after waking in the morning. After you clear out the mental fog, use the heel of one foot to massage the sole of the other foot. Really knead the muscles. Alternate between gentle and strong strokes. Use your heel to bend the toes forward and back. Pay attention and feel the benefit of this work. In the beginning, you may need to start gently, but after some practice, this morning massage will be one of the enjoyable parts of your day. Far from just helping you wake up, you'll find that you have more energy for those times when you need it most.

TOTEMS & SHAPESHIFTING

*A*nimals are a specific bundle of universal energy. Each animal carries a temperamental charge, representing a specific "personality" in the spectrum of existence. Repeated visitations by a particular type of animal often mean life is trying to tell you something. Alternately, a single powerful experience may also indicate an animal message destined for you.

It is well known that the body is an electromagnetic structure, and possesses areas of condensed energy called "centers" that mirror some of the main nerve plexi of the body. Energetic centers have correlations to medical meridians, psychic pathways, and outer phenomena. How these associations arise will become clearer later on. For now, let's stick to the basics.

The body maintains special arrays of bio-magnetic force called energy centers. Energy centers of the body are often compared with blossoming flowers. This comparison is due to the fact that when an energy center activates, it often feels like a flower blooming. If you have never felt the blossoming of a flower, don't worry, you will.

In some schools of shamanism, specific energy centers connect with a specific vision, a sound, or an animal. These associations are called totems. Despite differences in symbolism between the different schools, the effect is the same. Totems represent the way in which an archetypal quality interacts with the energy of the body to reinforce or educate the student on a quality they should develop. Occasionally, working with a specific totem will cause a fundamental shift in our potential. How far that shift goes depends on conditions, but that is the phenomena of shapeshifting.

Culture is the result of civilizations living and evolving under unique environmental conditions. The memories of this cultural experience are carried within the DNA and are recorded in the subtle energy patterns that permeate existence. The science of epigenetics is beginning to understand this interaction. Generally speaking, people from a particular cultural group have a history with a set of wisdom teachings (including totems) that are easily accessible to the shared state of community mind. For example, Native American totems tend to apply to Native Americans, whereas Tibetan totems tend to resonate most with individuals born near the Himalayas. As with all things however, this is a guiding principle, and there are exceptions.

When you have a chance, tune in with a meaningful totem, connect with that animal, be aware of its strengths and weaknesses, how it interacts with the balance of nature. Reflect on how its gifts may help you to notice your own special skills. As always, never forget that while animals are often bound by instinct, free choice reigns in humanity. Because of our freedom, we have great creative potential, but we need to nurture its balance.

With the teachings of the master shamans in mind, work with totems in order to promote balance and peace. It is possible to go down the opposite road, that of disturbance and conflict, but the consequences will be very severe. Life is a dynamic whole. If we act against life's balance, we breed tension, and that tension will eventually have an effect.

DISCLAIMER ON SHAPESHIFTING

*W*hen the ability to receive and respond to sensation is full, the body/mind becomes immensely calm, yet brimming with potential. *The veils between realms part.* In these moments, you will find that stillness happens naturally, and then the mind/body responds to the needs of life like the earth absorbing much needed rain. Of course, at other times, stillness will seem like a near impossibility.

Stillness is sometimes difficult. The body may twitch, or the mind may seem driven to move, although you are trying to be still! The conflict is astounding. One part of the mind battles against another, or so it seems.

The desire to move is sometimes the result of imbalanced pressure in an energy center. If you have never worked with energy centers, it's a hell of an adventure, and I only recommend study with a qualified teacher. Life can teach you in the absence of direct instruction, but there is value in having a teacher. Of great importance is recognizing the value of balance. Balance is key. Because energy centers are real, it is important to recognize how existence interacts with these dynamos of psycho-bio energetic force. Failing to deal with the reality of energy centers will tear you up.

The mind/body is full of inputs, including thoughts, emotions, habits, and choices, some of which we don't remember putting in. Some of them have been acquired unconsciously and others have been inlaid via media messaging, cultural conditioning, memories, hopes, fears, expectations or experiences from the past.

None of these are necessarily bad, but they must be seen for what they are. And yes, *some are bad for human life*, so be alert! Be mindful of how inputs affect our interaction with wholeness. The shaman must become clear with what is natural, individual human behavior compared to what comes as a result of socio-cultural conditioning. If this distinction is not made, the energy of the body goes awry and all manners of obstructions arise.

For shapeshifitng to occur naturally, without generating "negative karma," the energy centers must be balanced. For those who think shapeshifting is a Western phenomena and has no relation to karma, good or bad, I would recommend a closer study. What you find will amaze you.

Shapeshifting is one of many skills in the array of human potential. Shapeshifting often occurs with choice, but may occur spontaneously as well. In all cases, it's important to make sure the intention is correct. If not, the results may be quite undesirable. I'm not trying to make you gun shy. Shapeshifting is an important skill in the life of a shaman. And yet, the same code of conduct that goes into daily life must apply here as well. Esoteric skills must not be the hiding ground of the so called shadow self. In truth, there is nowhere to hide; there is no shadow separate from the light. In life, "there are not two," says the Brahma sutra, and it is precisely *because* there is no fragmentation that intention must be correct. If your intention is in harmony with the fullness of life, then shapeshifting will bring amazing goodness. We will return to shapeshifting later on.

SHAPESHIFTING:
Enhancing Sensation

It was cold, dark, and rainy. I sat in a place few visit even in good weather, and where no one comes on a day like this. It took a while to get to this quiet cove along the West side of the Hudson River. Finding it was rewarding. I was in a bad mood that day, and I knew that this was a place I could be alone in the quiet and renew. And so, I began with the cadence technique. This technique helps the student reestablish a real-time connection with the flow of the moment. Letting the past be the past and letting the unformed future exist, unpressured by expectation.

Sitting still, layer by layer, I felt the mind unwind. During the unwinding, different areas of my body teemed with energy or became cold according to the thoughts passing by, or the sounds going on around me. Sometimes I wanted to move, and when that happened, I moved. When the movement was finished, I returned to stillness.

Dark clouds let loose shimmering threads of different lengths. Silvery and fast, they shot from the sky, parting the water concentrically and then disappearing into its depths. With each fear I released, with every expectation I let pass, I could hear and feel more. My senses expanded, like stretching after a night of deep sleep. I heard many of the rain threads and felt them transform the river's surface. Once smooth and steely grey, the river became a syncopated array of cymbals, and visually, a riot of colors shot forth on this seemingly colorless day. The energy of intelligence unfurled like the circular waves on the river's surface, intersecting with others of the same.

"The wave reaches its limit and returns. Following the return is like the journey home," said Master Rick. Going out is exciting, but its fullness comes in returning home. When the doors of energy have a balance of the inward and the outward, shapeshifting may occur spontaneously. Even if it's not spontaneous, under the proper conditions, shapeshfting will reach its highest potential. With shapeshifting, you may pierce the veil of time, heal the past, present, or future, or achieve any number of things. As with everything, most of what happens hinges on choice, and so, choose wisely. For me, on this day, shapeshifting was not required. A river trout sprang from the water, announcing it was time to leave.

When you can be undisturbed, allow your senses to hear, see and feel the fullness of what is going on around you. Remain in a comfortable position. Your position relates to the Earth element; the energy you will channel relates to Water. Your intention relates to Fire, and your understanding of the need for this movement is Wind/Wood. If you are in alignment with the sacred, then your work will be blessed by grace, Metal. If not, many complications may arise. Ultimately, every gate is involved in this practice.

If you are sitting, feel the chair you are sitting on, feel the air draw in around your nostrils, a tiny hurricane. Be aware that for all the spectrum of light we see, there is infinitely more that we ignore. Integrating sensation is not the same as seeking stimulation. The ego and its agenda are often confused with what can and should be done. The ego is conditional, partial, and fragmented – although it has its place. Complete feeling, the outgoing and the return, teach us how to live, mapping potential, without destroying the foundations on which we depend.

MIND GATE SELF STUDY
Forms and Methods of Shapeshifting

Shapeshifting usually happens for one of two reasons. The first is to balance the energy of the individual. The second is to assist in the balancing of things that appear to be outside the self. Once the energy becomes full, shapeshifting may occur.

The truth is, we are all shapeshifting all the time, but we don't realize we are doing it. They key is to shapeshift mindfully and in harmony with the flow of life. That is why rhythm and timing are important. It is important to have the mind, body, and the rhythms of life engage and feed back with one another so that timing, form, and rhythm are in balance with the needs of the moment.

Shapeshifting is considered an advanced skill, and there are levels of greatness among masters. One practitioner may only possess the rudiments of the skill, but that may be enough. Still another may perform amazing feats and be of little more value to mankind. In all cases however, if your intention is strongly rooted in what benefits the wholeness of life, then your expression of shapeshifting will, more likely than not, be exactly what's required at exactly the right time. The analytical teachings of shapeshifting may be considered intellectual in nature, but in practice the method is definitively physical. Needless to say, both the study and practice should be initiated with an intention to balance the five elements of human life.

BODY GATE SELF STUDY
A Basic Method of Shapeshifting

*B*ecause all existence is made of the same fundamental building blocks, and because consciousness is inherent in that existence, it is possible to emulate the state of consciousness embodied in the many facets of existence.

Existence is an experience in capacity. The challenge is to maximize capacity while not harming the process on which we depend. All indigenous wisdom traditions stress the importance of this fact. As life develops, it takes a while to get to the place where life-changing choice is real. For example, no matter what it does, a lemur cannot choose to destroy the world. Humanity is different. Humanity is at that place. Our choices are real and, at least recently, we are not handling the responsibility well. Shapeshifting can be a way to reconnect with a fuller sense of relationship, and if employed well, can infuse balance into a world in desperate need of recalibration.

Watch a cat move

Cats emanate softness and sensitivity while at the same time owning tremendous power. Every step lightly touches the ground. Every step is aware. At the proper time, full weight is transferred onto the limb. A stalking cat demonstrates this movement well. If

you have never seen the big cats stalk, a domestic one will do. For all their domestication, there is great wildness in cats of any stripe.

Feline movement allows quick, sensitive changes of direction. As you observe the sensitivity of cats, reassess your own movements in life. Do you plod through your journey, nearly falling with each step? Or do you feel the ground before you, before you commit your weight? Everyone makes mistakes, but become aware of this. Embody this catlike experience. It is not that we should mentally and physically become cats, but rather, we should not lose the ability to express catlike precision.

Despite their tremendous power, cats know how to relax. Counterbalancing the intensity of the hunt, cats can easily drop into deep relaxation when the time is right. So much of insomnia is because we have forgotten how to drop into deep relaxation.

Watch a cat sleep
Learn to release the body into the mattress when you sleep. Try it on your favorite chair too. See how cats release tension and mold into the shape of where they sleep. A paw draped over a tree branch, or totally curled around a pillow – cats appear boneless. Dynamically, their center is never locked. There is always the proper relationship between center and periphery, and that's why they always land on their feet. Every now and then, try to do "human activities" with the feeling of catlike softness, structure, and precision. Don't allow excess tension to interfere with how the center feeds the limbs with energy. The more practice you get, the more you will see how useful this can be. This is a basic lesson on shapeshifting. There is more, much more. But this is good for now.

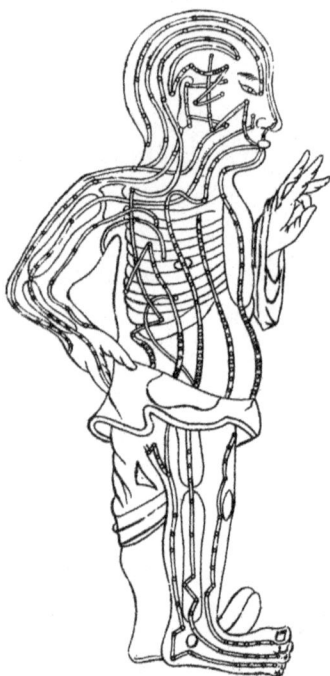

FIRE IN THE BLOOD

*F*ire was exploding within me. Master T.K. Shih wasn't moving. He was just sitting in front of me, his hand upon my wrist. His eyes were closed, and his fingers twitched upon my pulse points. With every passing moment, feelings of heat and movement became more pronounced.

"Everyone has a different sensitivity. Sensitivity is based on karma and practice. But now, you will feel the chi." Puzzled, I waited.

Progressively, the sensations I felt became stronger, as the feeling of chi grew. I didn't really know what chi was, but I sensed it was somehow connected to the rumors I had heard about this man. As I reeled in confusion, Master Shih began speaking, describing features of my life he had no obvious way of knowing. Stunned and amazed, I listened as he retold events that were significant in shaping my life – events he had no logical way of knowing.

"How can you know this?" I asked.

Simply, he replied, "I hear it in the chi."

Within only a few moments of touching my wrist, he knew I wasn't sleeping well; he knew I was anxious over my romantic relationship; and he knew that eight months earlier, I had undergone a medical ordeal that had shattered the world as I knew it. He told me much more, but, we will leave that for later. In 10 minutes, he had read my life as if it were a book. The odd thing was, he had just met me 10 minutes earlier. I had told him nothing of myself. Ever the skeptic, I had simply sat down, saying a friend recommended him to me. It was a grace that he clued me in at all as to what was going on. "Sometimes it is your destiny to know, sometimes it's not." So goes the advice I received from a close friend.

As I sat with Master Shih, with the scent of liniment heavy in the air, my shock turned to awe, as feelings of heat, chills and electricity coursed through my being. It was then I decided that I would find out what else this man could do. Furthermore, I resolved to determine how I could go about acquiring similar skills. According to the scientific method I had learned as a researcher, there was no rational explanation for how he could have known these things. I guess science needs to catch up with life. As of the time of this writing, I have known Master Shi for nearly a decade and the wonders he commands have not have not ceased. In the time I have known him, I have experienced things that can only be called miraculous. And he is not the only one who can do such things.

THE WATER RITUAL

*T*hroughout the ancient world, baths and bathhouses were used by shamans and lay people alike. The ritual of bathing provided a convenient way to interrupt the monotony of daily life while promoting the expansion of awareness – often leading to flashes of insight. Among the Asians, it was perhaps the Japanese who utilized bathing rituals more than anyone else. In the Occident, the Romans and Greeks deserved that distinction. Although bathing became very popular as a social custom, the original need for bathing was twofold. The primary need for bathing was hygienic cleansing. The second was as a rite of passage in the quest of vision. All ancient cultures and indeed all shamans have extolled the virtues and the needs of bathing. For individual insight, solitary bathing is most useful. For deepening the bond between lovers, bathing can enhance sensation, promote intimacy and be used to wash away stress. Free of stress, we may open more fully to one another, both giving and receiving more feeling, love and compassion. No matter how the bathing ritual is used, one must appreciate the significance of water, and how it may be used to good effect.

The famed Japanese *misogi* is an example of water ritual. It was used as a preparation for intense effort or to release the psychic grit and grime built up from hard practice. Misogi involves standing beneath a waterfall as the thunderous roar of water crashed about and all around you. One does not spend a particular period of time in misogi; the heart gives the indication as to when it is time to leave. Misogi can be an austere venture, and is not for the timid. For those who believe the misogi is too trying, there is the *onsen*, the hot spring spa. Useful results may also be gained by relaxing in the onsen but, the nature of the experience is entirely different. Misogi is the dynamic and relentless water ritual, with the aspiration that the dissolving power of water may remove the unhelpful attachments of ego, thus revealing the smooth glimmering diamond of soul within. When we step away from the roaring sound of falling water, we remember how small we are. Furthermore, sound is placed into perspective and we receive a fundamental experience of the spiritual sound of eternity.

Water cleanses, water soothes, and water in large bodies echoes the universal sound capable of enlightening souls in an instant. Baptism makes use of water, as does almost every ritual of any significance. There is power in water, and water responds to the heart. For proof of this, check into the work of Dr. Masaru Emoto. You will be amazed at what you find.

You may not have access to a waterfall, but you do have access to the mind. When needed, using your mind power, place yourself beneath the waterfall of your choosing. One day, you may sit beneath a gently cascading river, but on another day you may be beneath the roaring waters of Victoria Falls. Every now and then, use the misogi ritual. Allow the sonorous movement of water to drown out all your worries and roll away tensions of the body, mind and soul. I know one man who is adamant that he recreates the misogi in his shower. Then again, he says his showerhead is special. Put safety first, but why not give it a try?

BODY GATE SELF STUDY
Talking to Water

We have learned that all matter reflects and encodes the vibratory meaning of all existence. In fact, a string physicist went so far as to say that if we could understand the full reality of even one particle, the entire history of existence could be derived. The shamans show how this profound truth extends beyond the laboratory into our daily lives.

Composed of more than 70 percent water, the human body represents the many ways that thought and experience may be channeled so as to support the meaning and purpose of existence. Of great importance in this process is the function of consciousness. The importance of consciousness is all too often overlooked.

While scientists go on studying the predictable movements of material existence, they fail to identify the missing link that travels silently along with the photons and material waves. Consciousness infuses life with an endlessly responsive, creative potential. Working with the interplay of matter and mind, we make life all it can be and clear the path on the road to the meaning and purpose of life. One useful way for working with the power of intelligent interconnection is by blessing water, and then using the wave form of that blessing to enter your body and provide much needed renewal to your mind, body and soul.

The work of Masaru Emoto lends credence to the longstanding shamanic tradition of water blessings. In this self-study lesson we will provide you with the basic knowledge you need to perform water blessings on your own.

1. Prepare a glass of water. If possible, use drinkable, filtered water, but tap water is fine if filtered water is not available.

2. Using the cadence technique, calm your mind and focus your awareness on the intention of the ceremony. For example, if you are using this water to help support healing in the body, then bear this intention clearly in mind.

3. Hold the glass of water in your non-dominant hand. For example, if you are right-handed, hold the glass of water in your left hand.

4. Gently, place your dominant hand above the glass of water, palm facing down.

5. Dive deep into the moment. For however long is necessary, direct the heat and warmth of your upper hand into the water waiting in the glass below. Actually see that the water is receiving the energy and intention of your mind and encoding that information in its structure. When you feel the energy has been received and is encoded in the water, drink the water in three equal sips. When you are finished take a few moments to connect with the water passing through your body, and thank the water for performing its amazing functions.

Favored among many shamanic schools, this method can be used whenever you feel that water may help support deep healing in body, mind and soul.

FULLER PERCEPTION – TAI CHI CH'UAN

*I*n my Tai Chi classes, I often say, "It's a good thing we didn't wait for the doctors to confirm the benefits of Tai Chi. Otherwise, we'd be 400 years behind!"

A Center of Disease Control study found that elderly people who practice Tai Chi fall less frequently than those seniors who do not. In addition, Tai Chi practitioners break bones 50-percent less of the time if they do fall. According to the CDC research, Tai Chi offers great benefits – at the very least, keeping people on their feet. The creators of Tai Chi knew of its benefits 400 years before the CDC published their report. For the innovators of Tai Chi Ch'uan, the art not only made good medicine, it was good common sense.

"The root is in the foot," say the Tai Chi classics. Establishing the root of the foot is not only good for the legs, but for the heart and mind as well. To establish the root, to gain the powerful dynamic balance of Tai Chi, stiffness must be released. Releasing stiff tension allows the body to relax and this confers benefit systematically. "As you relax, you become less afraid, and as you become less afraid, the more you relax – This is the nature of progress," said Cheng Man Ching.

Tai Chi is primarily a method of the body gate. Plumbing the depths of the body gate, we discover things that have been close to us, but we have overlooked. So called "modern science," in its ambition to understand the far and the deep, has overlooked much of what lay under its nose. If we don't perceive fully with the tools that are close to us, then every piece of equipment we manufacture will measure "reality" with inherent imprecision. The effects of this are profound and disturbing. How much reality could be measured by those lacking in the most fundamental skills of being human? How many new innovations produced by minds unaware of themselves merely end up short-circuiting our humanity? By contrast, in being more sensitive to the full array of human experience, innovation can be enlightened, sustainable, and good for the balance of life.

Tai Chi promotes heightened sensitivity to the human body/mind. This sensitivity is often overlooked. Overlooking the sensitivity, we become awash in agitation and, as a result, experience fragmentation. Every student I have ever taught has always marveled at sensitivity rediscovered through Tai Chi Ch'uan. Some students release tension that was a drain on health; others improve athletic or sexual performance. Some students discover the mysteries of chi.

Tai Chi promotes awareness of wholeness via the sensory workings of the only tool you have: your body and mind. A fuller perception of wholeness may be the most precious gift the shamans can give us and may be the only thing to avoid wide scale destruction and loss.

SEXUAL BLISS

*D*espite the impermanence of life, despite the possibility of incredible sadness and suffering, there is beauty in life, and there is bliss. Many people believe that sex is one of the few activities that lead to pure, unadulterated bliss. It's not that simple. The integration of life provides that almost **any** experience *under the correct conditions,* may serve as rich food for enlightenment, bliss. Understanding the interplay of those conditions, however, is crucial. Under the wrong conditions, even the pursuit of bliss leads to suffering. Sex demonstrates this fact well.

In the spring of 2010, I finally succeeded in getting one of the most gifted teachers I've ever known to open up about a topic he usually avoids, sex. A traditionalist by nearly any definition, you'd never expect him to speak of it, let alone discuss how to magnify its pleasure! As a result, I was surprised when the Master spoke with tremendous honesty about the beauty and importance of sex. His talk wasn't graphic, it wasn't overly technical, but it was honest and pure. In fact, so pure was his elucidation that I almost felt embarrassed listening. I hardly made eye contact with him. It felt almost like inadvertently walking into a room when someone is reading a letter from a loved one far, far away. The purity of the person's emotion is so deep, you feel embarrassed to intrude. In this case though, sitting in front of the master, it was our duty to ask and learn, and his obligation to share what he could. And why should his wisdom not include these topics as well? A husband, father, octogenarian and qigong master of the highest level, this man is wise. We are lucky that he did speak, and I feel gratified to be able to present what I learned, here in this book.

There are techniques for magnifying the sexual bliss triggered by intercourse. We'll discuss some of them in other chapters. But there is something more important to discuss right now. Of more importance is the pairing between lovers. Just like a doctor must apply a treatment that matches the disease, sex between people who are not paired well only breeds suffering. The Master shook his head solemnly and offered an example.

"Young children are having sex now, it's terrible." Continuing, he said, "The energy, the mind of the children, is not stable, and they have sex, because they think it is OK. Sex too soon only confuses the body-mind. Sex at the wrong time only provides information that the structure cannot understand. It leads them into difficulty for a long time." Far from being moralistic, *which I totally expected*, the Master was speaking from the heart, about a special kind of hygiene most of us can't feel. Without this hygiene, we lose our soul. Sex at the right time is bliss, but sex under the wrong conditions leads to confusion and loss. It is the same for any specific type of action. Such is the nature of Tao, the natural way.

Sex can lead to tremendous bliss, but the conditions must be correct. The pairing must be correct, and the intention must be correct. Anything else may generate a short-term satisfaction lasting minutes, or hours, but eventually, the sensation ends. Eventually, an emptiness sets in. To avoid this, the heart withdraws, seeking substitution or numbness. And so it goes, until some event breaks the cycle. Alternately, if we can catch the mind in the moments leading to choice, we can choose well, and set a new pattern, perhaps a new pattern that leads to lasting happiness and bliss.

THE OPPOSITE OF LOVE
AND A WARNING FOR MANKIND

*T*he opposite of love is fear, and the fire of fear is self-loathing. Self-loathing is not relieved by adopting an "anything goes" mentality. At the same time, it doesn't mean that anything isn't possible. An old saying goes, "you can do whatever you want, but karma is carried on its back." Within the field of possibility, each of us has a role and a choice. Master Rick explained the roles and taboos of human- and animal-kind.

"Animal spirits must protect and reproduce. Humanity has a different role. Our job is to interact with life and creatively expand the divine wish." Shaking his finger at me, the master warned, "For this reason all the shamans learn from nature and never do something that goes against the fundamentals."

"Yeah, well, what about free will," I countered. *I must have suffered from temporary insanity.* What I said stunned Master Rick as much as it stunned me. What was I thinking?! Foolishly, I continued. "What about the choice to do something? Isn't *anything* possible?" My better sense finally caught up with me, I looked to the floor and waited for the worst.

With a stern voice, he began. "Yes, clever boy, anything *is* possible. I have seen people levitate and do amazing things. But, such things are only done at the right time and in the proper amount. One never forgets one's humanity when looking at the divine – or you fall. And fall hard." I sat with my jaw wide open, feeling like I had been eviscerated. Master Rick was unrelenting in his response to one of my ongoing complaints – specifically, that the mystic path is laden with so many behavioral taboos; I wondered how it was a path of freedom at all.

"Humility and the desire to work with the wisdom of nature are necessary. If you don't have this, don't study with me! Choice is applied in harmony with nature, not to inflate the ego. If you disagree, then go and study with someone else." Never before had I felt so alone. Even the thought of leaving him was frightening to me, and I'm sure it was all over my face. Without taking another breath, or so it seemed, he continued. I felt like the room closed in around me.

"The behavioral teachings are not about controlling. They are a guide with lessons contained within. Of course you can learn lessons by doing whatever the hell you want. Go play with a hornet and see what you get! People do much worse, and they get the fruit they deserve – if not now, then in time. This is unavoidable. The shamans are worried these days because people are forgetting their link with nature – forgetting the fundamentals. People think the pathways serve humanity. The pathways serve humanity only as much as humanity works for the harmony of nature. The pathways existed before humanity. Ignoring this, we cause disturbance, and that disturbance will be counterbalanced. Too much of this, and the results will be grave indeed." I have never heard Master Rick speak more passionately or issue a sterner warning.

MASTER RICK AND THE BEAVER DAM

*M*aster Rick was tall and thin. An athlete by nature, he discovered intellectualism late in his teens. Before that, his mind was too "caught up in nature," as he used to say. Because he was absorbed in nature more than textbooks, his early formal education was unremarkable. Fond of running in the woods or examining nature by remaining still while in it, his parents worried for his sanity, and doubted that his intellect would develop much at all.

Ironically, in conversation, he would often put the Ph.D.'s to shame. He had an incredible grasp of complex material and could make even the most menial of things a topic of fascination. While academia often lingers on the brink of impracticality, everything Master Rick said resonated as deeply true, both in theory and in practice. He was a model of a man embracing both the passionate and practical. In many ways, Master Rick was the opposite of me.

Despite my youthful love of nature, life had always been very abstract for me – until I met Master Rick. He was the root teacher who helped me reconnect with the parts of myself academia had made nearly silent.

Master Rick accepted few students. In fact, I only met one other student in all my years studying with him. "I don't want any recognition Robert, I don't want students. Teaching happens. I live my life and that's that. That's my way. Others should be teachers, but not me, not in a public way. That's why we've got people like you." Winking, he slapped me on the back. It was always unclear whether he meant things like that as a compliment or a derisive social commentary. I'll clarify.

One day, looking over the woody brush surrounding his house, his gaze stopped suddenly. Just beyond the tree line was a beaver resetting a branch on its home. South, just about 40 feet, was the beaver dam. Taking a deep breath, Master Rick whispered. "His productivity is with the cycles of nature. What he does will not destroy the fundamental flow of life here on Earth. What he does allows the smaller cycles to carry on, and allows the larger cycles to turn in course. Often, what we do destroys the human realm and impairs the ability for energy to flow in the other realms as well. The fact that we even need teachers is an indication that we are far from the effortless way. Far from nature. Far from ourselves." Suddenly he became even more serious.

"There are two ways to learn. One grows you in the process, the other, destroys you." He looked like a dragon. Long hair coursing down his shoulders. Steam spiraled out his nose and drifted into nothingness. He really looked like a dragon. Drawing in again, he continued.

"Ideally, people don't need shamans. Ideally, we are all in tune with nature. Ideally, we do not 'work' nature to achieve anything. What we do improves our ability to express life and lets others do the same. It's not a matter of interpretation. It's as clear as this. Some people like to blur the lines with convoluted theories. That's the first sign of deception. Look at this simplicity, Robert; that's the power and grace of nature. Moving mountains, naturally in harmony with nature; gradual movement, one branch at a time."

THUNDER FALLS LIKE RAIN

Thunder falls like rain
Rain strikes the ground
    as if fired from a thousand cannons.

Before God, the large is diminished,
the small is seen for its greatness
and beyond all that . . .
all things be
as they are

Words run backwards into muted puddles

Sight folds into itself

Sensation unfolds. . .
exposing the one light within

within

(the whispering. . . one singularity)

sssshhhrrrrrrrrrrrrrr

Court the gentleness of your breath
follow gently, patiently,
be calm
be peaceful

In total peace,
a calm wind,
will still the lake shores of your mind.

Once settled, your attachments to that will be freed.
and deep into the lake, or into the boundless sky
you see
is but one

Sea of mind.

feel the rain which moistens your soul

THE LAMA'S GLOW

I work with a man who says he's always been able to see auras. Although I can make them out, I don't have the skill he has. But I find the skill intriguing. Auras are one of those things that I probably wouldn't believe in if I hadn't witnessed so many other strange events. Many of those direct experiences are recounted all throughout this book. In the end, piece it together for yourself. Therefore, while I leave the door open for people having the skill, I can't say I have achieved significant proficiency in the art. But my colleague is another matter.

One Sunday in the summer of 2010, my colleague and I were receiving an empowerment under the revered Lama Norlha Rinpoche. Almost unknown to many spiritual seekers, Lama Norlha Rinpoche is not part of the spiritual supermarket and wasn't even known to be a Rinpoche until the information was leaked out, years after his arrival in America. Previous to the revelation, he had quietly conducted his duties, never insisting upon any special recognition. If you have the chance to meet Lama Norlha Rinpoche, you'll get a sense of this peaceful, magnanimous man.

During the ceremony, I couldn't help but notice my friend oddly turning his head as if he were checking his eyesight. His movements were genuinely disturbing. I wasn't sure if he was squinting to get a better view or if he might be suffering from heatstroke. For a while I considered asking him about it, but decided against it. He's an eccentric type (aren't we all?). And so, I left him to his adjustments and paid attention to the powerful sensations rocking my body like so many waves on some turbulent shore.

What I (and others), experienced during that ceremony was amazing. So profound was the event that I completely forgot about my friend's gyrations. Finally, hours later, he started the conversation. I'll retell it here and leave the rest to you.

"You know how I've mentioned that I can see auras?" he asked.

"Yeah, I know," I answered. "Well, usually, most people have auras that reach about an inch or two off the surface of the skin. As you know, I don't really see the colors yet, but I can see the shine. And for most people, the auras don't go out very far. But today, I noticed something I couldn't believe. I could tell you were annoyed by how I was moving, but I just had to be sure. I was trying to make sure I was seeing what I *thought* I was seeing."

"Well, give it up already; what did you see?" I interjected.

Well, you know that part when Lama Norlha Rinpoche began making the hand gestures and actually reciting the prayers? Well, his aura was at least one and a half feet extended all around him. It wasn't just this haze like most people have; his aura was like fire glowing in the room. I've never seen anything like it." We raised our eyebrows, shook our heads, and felt lucky to have been there.

Truly, there are so many amazing stories about the high-level lamas. Although I can't see auras well, knowing what I do about Lama Norlha Rinpoche, tells me this story is not only possible, it's probable.

Lama Norlha la Chaktsal (Homage to Lama Norlha Rinpoche!)

CONTINUUM EFFECT

"All people have Grandfathers' grace. All of us have a special medicine. For many reasons, some people do not use their medicine. Sometimes it's blocked by pain, sometimes it's blocked by ignorance. Sometimes it's blocked by harming Mother Earth. The more people can learn about the power of their medicine, they will be careful not to take on things that stop their medicine's development."
– Native American Elder

*T*he basic tools of shamanism are the basic operations of life. All the miracles we seek must make their way into the human realm to be perceived. If there are major blockages in the heart, mind, or body, it makes it more difficult for the miraculous to enter into one's life. This fact is often overlooked. Our state of mind has much to do with the expression of miracles. This is both the gift and the curse of free will.

In Africa, there is a saying: "A blessing cannot come without the individual soul's *(ori)* consent." That is to say, the individual seeking help must open his heart to allow help to come in. If one wishes to become less angry, one must release the clenched fist. Only then can the hand of friendship be received.

There are many miracles we never see. They are shimmering just above the mind's awareness of them. Having their root in spirit, they descend through the limbs of existence, and rest at the level permitted by the spirit or soul of the individual. Just as miracles happen, big and small, comprehensive and diminutive, so too are the powers of the shaman expressed along a continuum.

One shaman may excel at one type of work while another may have skill in something altogether different. It's all based on karma, acquired characteristics. I knew a shaman who was born without the sense of smell. He has never known the aroma of citrus or the velvet softness of lavender. Despite his "lack," there are few who can match his healing touch. A gifted and talented healer, he affects cures others cannot reach. We are all unique. We must not allow perceived shortcomings to hinder comprehensive development. The shaman seeks to develop wide and deep to ensure that dispensation of spirit has full play in our lives.

IN THE BEGINNING, IT WAS NATURAL

*I*n the beginning, people lived in balance with life. Ages ago, there was no need for medicinal herbs, no need for special exercise, and no need to focus on maintaining a connection with grace. Long ago, we were humble enough to be with God without interruption. Long ago, life changed, and there was a reason.

The student asks,

"Rabbi, it is said that in the past, people saw the face of God. Why isn't it so anymore?"

The teacher answers, "Nowadays, no one can stoop low enough."

May I call that humility?

Times have changed.

When people use their bodies correctly, and work in harmony with nature, the organs are cleansed, the muscles exerted, and respiration is deep and full. The brain thinks and feels in equal measure. After all, there are two hemispheres to the brain, aren't there?

When we are being in balance, the nerves are strong and at peace. Food is prepared according to the seasons, and medicinal herbs are the flavorful elements of what is enjoyed each day. Of course, that was long ago.

More than 20,000 years ago, wise kings noticed a degradation affecting humanity. The cause of that degradation was great indeed. And at that time the so called "components" of healthy living were devised. Intended to be a bridge to naturalness, it was not long before the descent of mankind's mind made environmental differences the subject of ego fragmentation, bigotry and hate. And yet there is a benefit in that contraction. Because the world is growing smaller each day, we are forced to see that naturalness is the only hope to save our relationship with this planet, and true love the only relationship that is real.

Perhaps in time, we will see the deeper meaning of the five elements and the three gates. And then in recognizing and realizing the essence we will draw close to the naturalness itself. It is inexpressible but identifiable, powerful and compassionate, comprehensive but relevant to the needs of our global family. Every natural thing is composed of such self-evident truthfulness: air, water, love, and life.

SHAMANIC STAGES

*G*enerally speaking, progress involves five steps. First, the mind is made clear. The direction of study should be defined. Next, the body capacity is made strong enough for shamanic work. Third, the pathways of wisdom are taught, and fourth, they are explored according to the nature, disposition and need of the apprentice. At all points along the way, one is mindful of the supreme power and alert to learn from its presence in nature. That relationship to grace is the fifth factor, unbounded by time. More than anything else the student is reminded that life is not man made, and to that eternal force that human ego must bend in humility. Failing to harmonize with nature leads to tragic results for the soul no matter how a person's lifestyle appears before death.

Not all schools of shamanism follow this rule directly, but in some form or another, the process exists. The goal is harmony with the inherent intelligence of creation. It goes without saying that there are more and less accurate expressions of the path. One must be honest about what type of energy one is using in one's study of life. "Ye shall reap what ye sow," said the Nazarene. Similar sentiments are echoed in all our wisdom traditions. We cannot escape the energetic effects of karma, although the intensity of karma received may be adjusted.

Invariably, when people think about karma, questions of life and death, illness and health come to mind. For example, how is it fair when a child is born in this world and faces difficulty? Children are so vulnerable, they have done nothing wrong. Why is it that they suffer? These are important questions. We will deal with them more fully later on. But for now, consider this. In some cases, the child really is innocent. In some cases, a child's misfortune stems from the poor decisions of the adults who have formed the world into which the child was born. If we adults lose touch with relationship and, as a result, increase danger in our world; it is only natural that the most vulnerable will suffer. Then, as those children acclimate to an increasingly painful world, they may learn to project that pain onto the next generation. And so on, and so on. This is the nature of degradation. Such degradation must not continue unchecked. If we are to proceed in the shamanic, we must clean up our internal environment and the one outside us as well. After all, we cannot escape the fruits of our actions. It is a spiritual and scientific fact: the universe catches us . . . whether in this life or the next.

UNION WITH THE DIVINE

*W*e are never separate from the source of life. In some way the beginning of the path is also the end. The moment we realize – really deeply realize – that the unity in life means we cannot be separate from its source, then, in that moment, life changes completely. We may not totally leave our imperfections behind, but in recognizing our fundamental connection with the source of all things, we are at least aware that there is a way to peace.

"Life is not man made" said Bruno Groening. Life is *not* man made; life issues from eternity. These fundamentals are the source of the existence. Sadly, we all too often think that human life, that consciousness itself, is some aberration of probability. No, consciousness exists, because the totality is conscious, and this totality is God.

If this understanding settles deep within us, permeates our thoughts and feelings, then we will know without a shadow of doubt that conscious intelligence is the substance of all existence. If we are not pressured by habituation, if we are allowed to naturally think about and sense this truth, then we will reclaim the universal birthright of an intimate, aware, and therefore full relationship with the source of all things. The irony of human life is that within the narrow parameters of one conscious lifetime we seem to have the ability to deny the very fundamental basis of what we are. This is truly a case of being scared by our reflection in a still moonlit pool. We are reflected everywhere.

The grace of existence is ever present in full measure. For

many reasons, people go through stages of availability to that ever present grace. One student was beaten as a child, and so, physical practice, the pre-requisite strengthening of the body, was difficult for him. As a child, if he "caused trouble," his father forced him to stay in a push-up position for long periods of time. As a result, his shoulders developed arthritis later in life. In his physical body (and the mental one), there were blockages that were difficult to overcome. In his case, we worked around it. We strengthened other parts of his mind/body. Then, when the energy was full, we returned to the shoulders. Naturally, we found them much improved as compared to the beginning. He is making great progress in his availability to the fullness of being.

As we proceed in dissolving blockages of body and mind, the student finds that his or her availability to grace becomes more present in daily life. Also, in times of meditation, the physical or mental techniques become a gateway to a deep absorption with the universal energy. The Essene said "Man cannot live on bread alone, but depends on every word that comes from the mouth of God." In the beginning, was Logos, "Word," the very vibratory structure of existence. This vibration exists still and is known as the Holy Spirit, the Rauch (Hebrew), the Universal Energy, the Witness of Creation, or the Taraka Brahma which meets us in the exact capacity we need to sustain the dance. If we are capable of only one step with the Divine, then in that step we shall be met. If we may remain enthralled for longer periods of time, then in that depth we shall swim, and emerge renewed.

IN THE BEGINNING

*T*he total consciousness, the source of all things, made a movement long ago to express existence along certain pathways. Human life is one of those pathways of existence. Naturally, there are many more. Plants, animals, bacteria, even inorganic matter represent some of the lines of existence that issued forth from the source of all things. There are lines of existence we know about, and many of which we are generally unaware. The shaman excels in relating to the many lines of existence. Any of us may employ the shaman's art, if we are willing to accept the responsibility that goes along with it.

Each thread of existence has its own way for expressing its full potential. That is to say the way a fly expresses its full potential is not the way a human should conduct his or her life. First and foremost, humans have no wings. It is important that each living thing express its full potential while not unduly restricting the ability of others to do the same.

Human life is a process in which awareness of our life interacts with our free choice in how we move through life experiences. Despite recent rapid technological developments, the essence of humanity has not changed much at all. As a result, there is a vast body of information that can serve as a roadmap for our journey of life. It is remarkable that all ancient sages agreed on the nature of what best serves the development of full human potential.

In general, the ancients recommend we take care of hygiene,

that we move according to nature, that we utilize resources sustainably, that we respect our teachers, seek healthy relationships and that finally, remain ever open to the intercession of the grace of life itself. According to the ancients, balancing these elements results in an alchemical process, one that enhances our availability to the fullness of life. We are told that if we persist, we will arrive at the palace of the eternal. The many tools of the shaman are meant as a reference point in assessing our relationship to the wholeness of life. All the teachings, all the methods, are to serve an optimal healthy relationship between existence and our relationship to Grace. Anything else is absurd, because everything is connected.

Explore the interplay of action and grace. Strive for a harmony that allows life to unfold in full harmony. Doing so is immensely creative and will leave you with a clean heart. Throughout life such a clean heart is a tremendous benefit. Even if we don't feel clean in the beginning, even if we are not perfect – no one is – drop by drop, choice by choice, we can minimize the effect of errors and make our way back to peace. This is the nature of human life. All tools of shamanism work to support availability to Grace. Just use them wisely. Explore this connection in all you do and, eventually, you will consciously abide in the all-fulfilling relationship available to us all.

HATSUMI'S BIG TOE

One of the simplest and most accessible ways to build the energy of the body is through movement. The sages in the past discovered this truth and encoded the wisdom of intelligent movement in the systems that would become Tai Chi, yoga, shapeshifting, and therapeutic massage, among others. The good thing about movement is that anyone can do it. The bad thing is that, depending on your level of fitness, some types of movement may be totally out of the question. It is important to find a system that works for you and then develop your potential.

One evening about six years ago, one of my chi gung teachers began teaching some rather obscure types of chi gung, or energy movement, to about 20 of us in Woodstock, New York. The sets ranged from the sophisticated to the absurd. The unique and colorful sets bore names such as "The Matchmaker," "The Flying Crane," and "The Walking Cow." To anyone looking in from the outside, we must have been quite a sight.

As he often did, the Master ended our session with a guided meditation. Right before he started, though, he mentioned something as an afterthought. I've asked a number of students about this since then, but only one, even vaguely remembers the reference. Nonetheless, the method is recorded in my notes, and it's not the kind of thing I would have mistaken. Still, for about six years, it bugged me that no one else really remembered the informal exposition. The method is so simple that it might easily be missed, and apparently was. I've practiced the method every day since then, but had a bit of doubt in my mind as to whether I had misunderstood totally.

Finally, in the summer of 2008, I was re-reading one of my favorite books, when I discovered Dr. Masaaki Hatsumi's reference to the method that I learned taught many years earlier. Just then a veil lifted. Suddenly, I remembered an independent bit of information I learned from Master Shi during one of our acupuncture training intensives. In the class, Master Shi described how the liver and gall bladder meridians traverse the length of the body. Thus, if one can exercise just these two meridians, then the health of the body can be powerfully supported.

The essence of it is this: Whenever possible, move the big toe – just the big toe. Develop the dexterity so that you can lift, lower, and rotate both big toes without moving the rest of the toes or the feet. Use sets of 36 repetitions. If in the beginning you can't do it, then use your hands to manipulate the toe. Eventually, get to the point where you move just the toe. This method works because the ascending liver meridian passes near to the descending pathway of the gall bladder. As both liver and gall bladder are important for rejuvenation, this one method powerfully supports the recuperation of body and mind. Finally, because the spleen meridian also relates to the big toes, digestion and energy exchange are enhanced as well. I work on this practice the moment I wake up, while I'm lying in bed. I've been doing it for years and have never been disappointed. Enjoy!

CONSCIOUS UNIVERSE

Consciousness pervades existence.
The truth of this is easy to prove.

As human beings we make choices. We think, we feel, and we respond. While all of this is happening, we are made of the same atoms – the same fundamental material as the entire universe.

And here's the part some people try to deny: If the human body is the seat of intelligence and consciousness *and* is made of the same atoms as everything else, then there must be consciousness everywhere. Do you see that point? If there is consciousness emerging from your atoms, then where does it end? Perhaps it doesn't.

To deny the reality of consciousness embedded in nature is to deny the most fundamental parts of ourselves. How can we find the meaning of human life if we deny the basis of our being? If we don't recognize the fundamental unity of mind and matter, everything else is prone to error. For this reason, all the shamans advise, "know thyself." Know that there is no mind/body split. There is not and has never been a mind-matter split! Matter is mind in form. As is eloquently stated in the Brahma Sutra: "there are not two." Do not miss the importance of this!

THE SURGEON FROM GUANGZHOU
Part 1 of 2

*M*aster Liu pressed so hard I almost passed out. But when it was over, the pain was gone. I'm not kidding. I had been pale, and bent over for two days. The pain had been dizzying. And then, within moments, the pain was gone. As unbelievable as it sounds, it's true. Within moments of her touch, the pain was gone, and it never returned.

"How is that you can do these things Master Liu?" I asked. With a genuine but calm grin, she replied softly, "I can't do anything. Life set the pattern. I'm just using my natural function. I learned to develop rare skills that most people ignore. Overall, we are too distracted from naturalness. We miss what is obvious. Each of us has our own distraction, and also our own way back." She continued, "Part of my distraction was my power as a surgeon."

"I used to be a surgeon in Guangzhou. I used to have *every* privilege. You can't imagine the lifestyle I lived. If I wanted something, I would snap my fingers, and there was someone to give it to me. I saved people's lives – *powerful people*. And they wanted to reward me."

"At the same time, I was seeing every kind of suffering. And then, I met my Master and began to learn this art. This art gives me so much joy, because I help heal problems before they get bad. But it's not that I'm anything special. Anyone can do this, if they use the body battery correctly. There are secrets to the body and to human life that most people never see. But when you find a real master, like my teacher, then you realize what you've been missing." "So tell me," I continued, "How did you learn? You started as a medical doctor; how did it happen?"

Now, working on my foot, she pressed hard again. The pain was tremendous! I wondered, "Why does she keep doing that?" Odd it seems that when she gives me pain, my pain is relieved? Payment for a shortcut I suppose. Smiling at the question, she answered.

THE SURGEON FROM GUANGZHOU
Part 2 of 2

"When everyone else was dating or partying, I was practicing chi gung. I was inspired by the idea of helping people. I saw people suffering so much, in so many ways, I wanted to help. I had a good motivation, and it made me work hard. The hours I spent . . . the work, was not easy. At times I thought these skills were fake. Depending on your mental and physical blocks, certain skills come sooner or later. And, in addition to that, there are so many fakes. As a student you need as much luck as persistence."

"In my case, I had seen my master heal amazing problems, and, as a surgeon, I knew it was real. So, I gave it a shot. First, my master said I needed to regain my natural functions first – the basics of being human. We lose so much in "growing up." We assume that we need to kill or suppress one part in exchange for another. It's just not true. All we need to do is keep growing healthfully. Goodness always supports more goodness. In time, we begin to feel again, the full feeling, like when we were children.

"As a doctor I learned to use special tools and to think in a very specific way. But that specific thinking closed down other functions. In fact, some doctors even believe that acupuncture and chi are useless. But they could not deny the results. Eventually, they either ignored me, or came to study with my teacher. It is strange to see people walk away from what is good, only because it makes them uncomfortable. Anyway, I learned to see the balance.

"Depending on the injury, I might do surgery, but other

problems, only the chi can reach. We must be able to change tools as needed. But no tool should cause a loss of natural function," said Master Liu.

With that one statement, Master Liu clarified an important point. In some cases, as she asserted, "technology represents a loss of function." If we lose the function for too long, it becomes an imbalance.

Master Liu continued, "If the imbalance remains too long, it can be very difficult to correct. Surgery or medications will try to reach it, but it's too deep. By the time we use surgery, the mind has often accepted the neurological memory of disease. Treatment must enter the deep layers of mind and emotion. In an instant, people must feel the bliss of natural happiness. Then the body can "reset," and there is a chance to heal from the inside out. Using both ways together is our method. We are intelligently open-minded." I am reminded of some time I spent with the nephew of a good friend.

During a visit, the boy told me he could play tennis very well. Looking around, I asked where his tennis racket was. He told me he didn't have one. I was puzzled, but then I saw the entertainment console. Instead of a racket, he had a wand.

"You should try the real thing" I said, "It's more fun."

Rather disparagingly he answered, "Real tennis is too hard, this is better." Already forming a plan, I smiled.

In the Spring, I plan to take him out so we can play real tennis. And when we go, I'll do everything I can to make real tennis more fun than pixels on a screen. Outside, we'll play hard and laugh when I secretly let him win points that he thinks he has no chance of winning. We'll use our senses to track the ball, and adjust moment by moment to a real ball, really flying through the air. Dr. Liu's words come to mind. "No tool should cause a loss of natural function". Although I did enjoy playing virtual tennis, I look forward to the time when I can help my young friend enjoy the real world, at least as much as the digital. After all, we are human, and living in the real world is natural.

(Eight months later)

Last week, the boy and I played tennis. Afterward, he said to me, "Uncle Rob, when it's raining, I'll use the computer. But whenever it's sunny, I'd like to play tennis outside with you and my friends. My arm hurts a little, but it was a lot of fun."

The pain of growth is different than the pain of disuse. The pain of growth actually makes us happier, rebalances error and helps maintain a connection to the joy of living. *Set point for natural functioning!*

THE BEGINNING AND THE END

Years in the desert
Dormant
One drop of water,
The seed cracks open

MIND GATE SELF STUDY
Reliance in Grace

Please remember
Remember frequently
That life is not man made

Yes, it's true that men and women are able to observe life – to think
about life.
Yes, life gave humanity the ability to know and reflect – it's not the
other way around.
Our awareness of reflection did not create our ability to reflect and
know.

Our awareness is second to the development of existence.
We are made of forces that made us, the forces that made us are
not the "I"
We are not superior to life "outside" of us in anyway shape or form.

There is nothing outside,
There is nothing inside,
There are not two

Our reflections are close to the creative, but not the essence itself.
Life is not man made.
Life is not woman made.

For all our creations, the doer, the "I," is a fragment of eternity,
A necessary one, and we are aware of this.
We are well served to strive ardently for our highest purpose.

And always keep our senses open to the intercession of that mysteries force which made matter sheath the ability of intelligence to grow and look back upon itself. Ride that wave to the source and have faith in that – let this knowledge wash you in brilliance.

It is truly undeniable.

Shamanic principles are not the hiding place of egoism. They are not the foundations of ideology or bigotry. They are simply reminders drawn from direct verifiable, repeatable experience, for how each one of us can manage our relationship to grace – emerging from a group of people in distant places at distinct times, reminds us of what is found in being available to the wholeness of being. Don't twist it, or yourself, into what it is not capable of being. That is the seed of neurosis, delusion. In Sanskrit, this is called *maya*.

LIFE FORCE, MIND,
AND THE ROOT OF EXISTENCE

*A*ncient people believed the world to be full of a living energy. According to my teachers, this living energy is bio-active and travels through the nerves. In fact, the nerves have formed in order to carry this potent form of energy. This fact should not surprise us. After all, the entire body is made of positively and negatively charged elements. In fact, our thoughts require this electricity in order to express movement, communication, and in order to sense things from the environment. The body structures are made of atoms, and those atoms possess electrical charge. The nerves work because of electrical charge. Consciousness and bio-active electricity intermingle in the material world. Consciousness and bio-active electricity follow one another like fire and heat. If we allow this understanding to hit home, we see that the entire world, all existence, is awash in this flow of attractive and repulsive charge. How did it ever get started?

After the inception of existence, matter spewed forth from the creative seed and began discrete developments. Heavier matter developed differently than the lighter matter. Antimatter and fine matter interchanged in the dance of creation and destruction. All of this was known to the ancients, and has been going on long before we ever had words to describe it. Only recently has modern science come to see its reality. As matter began its march of expression, time and space sprang into being. The three-fold interaction of matter, time, and space began to organize the early elements into networks of possibility. Some matter became stars; other bits of matter follow a different path. As the winding road of destiny unfurled, matter arranged according to its conditions. From the atomic soup, matter began to congeal, interact, and form new and complex combinations. These combinations set a course of development until the organization became so complex, with enough material gathered unto itself, that the original unity of form and consciousness manifested once again! This dawning of consciousness appears random, yet it is supremely purposeful while being imbued with choice.

It is said that humanity has a mind. And so it is. We do have consciousness, don't we? And yet we are made atoms. All existence is seething with consciousness, isn't it?

Life is now looking back at itself through human eyes. It is carried on reflective, contemplative consciousness. When this phenomena occurs in harmony with the process which allowed for its potential, men and women become the so-called "sons and daughters" of God, or enlightened beings. When life abuses this ability of reflective consciousness either by wish, ignorance, or blind habituation, we say that person has "fallen." The individual is lost in delusion. Sometimes we fall and rise many times. Many times we do so in what appears to be one life; many times in what appears to be many lives.

As the primordial matter began its long course of development, each discrete pathway of potential found a set number of ways to interact with the rest of existence. This trend holds true until matter and consciousness intermingle in the miraculous. This is evidenced in the lives of the saints of our global shamanic traditions. Reflective contemplative awareness illuminates the connection between the ground of existence, its power of potential expressed in nature, and the miracle of the mind that may behold it!

AN AMERICAN SHAMAN
The Natural Philosopher,
George Washington Carver

*T*he magic and power of plants never escaped George Washington Carver. Born in the deep south in the late 1800's, struggling against the inequities of racial discrimination, Carver found freedom amid the greenery of the natural world.

The young Carver was fond of spending vast amounts of time in the wilderness, kneeling down, investigating the smallest details of plants. Time spent in deep silence made the young Carver alert – not only to the form of a plant, but to the many ways it interacts with the environment. This "network effect" consumed Carver, and, in fact, led to a hundreds of his discoveries relating to crop rotation, soil conservation, and crop utilization.

Carver believed it was his duty to utilize his skills to unfold the mysteries of "God's little workshop." Once those mysteries were unraveled, his greatest aspiration was to share the benefits of them with others. The many practical discoveries of Carver are well known. Interestingly, what is not well known is the intensely spiritual way Carver approached his studies. Carver believed that knowledge was a spiritual quest and its end was to benefit the world. He believed humanity was supposed to steward the gifts of God. For all his exceptional intelligence, Carver humbly assumed credit for his discoveries. His greatness was not merely of his own doing. His greatness came from the proper coordination of his skills with the divine wish. A story he told highlights this point well.

According to the story, Carver asked the Great Creator, "Dear

Mr. Creator, please tell me what the universe was made for." The Great Creator answered, "You want to know too much for that little mind of yours. Ask for something more your size." Then he asked, "Dear Mr. Creator, tell me what man was made for." Again the Great Creator replied, "Little man, you still are asking too much. Cut down the extent of your request and improve the intent." So then he asked, "Please Mr. Creator, will you tell me why the peanut was made?" Hundreds of important discoveries followed.

Another quote from Carver will do well to establish this man not only as an exceptional academician, but a botanist shaman of the highest order.

> *"I want them to see the Great Creator in the smallest and apparently the most insignificant things about them. How I long for each one to walk and talk with the Great Creator through the things he has created."*

Let us bend low and listen well. Let us join that conversation and realize, as Carver did:

> *"...there are scientist to whom the world is merely the result of chemical forces or material electrons. I do not belong to this class."*

In finding out why Master Carver did not belong to that class, we will come close to the meaning and purpose of life itself.

THE POWER OF TOUCH

"Massage is very important; the skin is very important." Master Liu prompted me to turn over as she spoke. Massage is one thing, but the beating I was getting was quite another. Her fists pounded my back, arms, and legs. Punishment, this might have been, but a massage it was not. Trained as a physician in China, Master Liu earned her stripes as a trauma surgeon. I was convinced I would need one! Nonetheless, I had faith in the woman. I knew her long enough to know that if she was hitting me, I damn well needed it. Beyond Western medicine, she has skills that border on the miraculous – All the more reason I submitted myself to the benefits of her blows. Through a sly grin, she maintained I needed the treatment to prevent "blockages of energy."

Twelve feet of nerve fibers are coiled inside one square inch of skin. Housed in a depth of only a few centimeters, the nerves of the body are packed tight and form an impressive grid. This array captures sensation and transmits feeling to the central nervous system. If the skin and its transmissions are not working well, myriad problems result. That's what is called a blockage.

Blockages come in all shapes and sizes. Sometimes a blockage begins with the mind and manifests in the body; in other cases, a bodily imbalance affects the quality of mind. Western science has proven this connection. Thankfully, touch can be one of the most powerful means for releasing blockage.

Generally speaking, the nature of a blockage determines the

153

type of touch required to release it. Bodily tensions may be categorized by the resistance they afford. For example, a stiff muscle may feel like a tight rope or be immoveable as stone. Each condition requires a unique intervention. Sometimes tension in one place causes a weakness elsewhere. In those cases, a specialized combination of massage is required. Touch can be used to ameliorate imbalance, but so too can needles, herbs, or carefully chosen words. In work like this, relationship is critical.

Touch is the meeting of two minds and two souls through the intermediary of physical contact. If the relationship is not correct, then the power of touch will be decreased. As important as techniques are, most important is intention. Each one of us is a powerful sender of nonverbal information. This information is stored in the way we manage tension and relaxation. Those who house tension in the mind cannot help but show it in the way the feel, literally the *way* they *feel*. Those who maintain poor bodily posture cannot help but stifle metabolism, crumple nerves, and promote the formation of mental and physical blockages.

With a single touch, muscles fibers release stiffness and powerfully shift cellular metabolism. Through touch, we can literally transform biological reality. Touch can relieve pain and provide us with experiences of bliss, energy, and inspiration. Actually, however, we don't need to be told this information. We already know the benefits of touch. And so, the way we hold our posture and the way we hold our hearts affect the quality of contact we receive, and allow us to give only the best.

"IT TAKES WORK TO FAIL"

*I*n college, there were few things I enjoyed more than spending a few hours shooting the breeze with Dr. Stanley Becker. One of the most interesting men I have ever met, he possessed a brilliant mind and had a set of life experiences to match. As well, he was something of an eccentric.

A combination of many rare things, he worked in many fields. He had been a teacher, a researcher, an outdoorsman, and was fluent in things mystical. His initial impression fooled you. He seemed to be too simple, too straightforward – even aloof. Only the daring received the gems this man protected from the masses. For those who endured the pressure of criticism, true academic criticism (never delivered cruelly), gems of insight and wonder appeared. Of all the academicians I've known, he, foremost among them, brought honor to the title, "Professor."

Becker was a storehouse of knowledge, and his simple thoughts utterly transformed the way you looked at things. , He was amazing, and although he was unapproachable to most, he was not to me. Sadly, most never bothered to get to know the treasure of his knowledge.

One day, perched on the wooden chair next to his desk, I mused pessimistically about a recent academic failure. Sunlight filtered through the blinds and made him look like a shadow. The same sun artfully illuminated the dust in his office, making it seem like a million tiny diamonds. Diamonds they were, strewn across the artifacts of knowledge. His was true knowledge: the art and science of things, life-changing insight – not the tawdry information sought by so many of today's charlatans. My thoughts were on my exam. I shook my head, wondering how I might save my grade point average.

"It's early in the semester, Robert. Forget the GPA. You know, Robert, it takes work to fail, *extreme* work. To fail, you have to *really* try. You have to be absent from class as much as possible (physically or mentally), because even just sitting there, about 20 percent of information will get in. Over time, that 20 percent builds and you'll probably pass. No, you have to *really* turn off common sense, and *really* distract yourself so that you do other things, instead of the things that you have time to do. So, you see, it really takes energy and effort to deny the effort required in the class *you chose*. And if you didn't choose it, you probably shouldn't be there anyway. So, it's really not failing. But you, Robert, you don't work hard to fail, you just need to find your way to succeed."

He was right. Not just about my class, but about everything. It takes tremendous energy to turn away from the wholeness that will help us be happy, healthy, and sound. It takes energy to deny the good things that are all around us. It takes energy to deny the people that, in our heart, we know are good for us, even though we avoid them out of fear they'll draw us into the happiness we're convinced we must deny, literally, to succeed at failure. It takes tremendous effort to turn away from the place our heart needs to be.

"The most unhappy people often work the hardest," said Swami. "They have to." The only way you won't discover these truths is if you decide to fail, if you decide not to look and if you decide to deny the truth of what you are. It takes work to fail.

PROOF OF THE SPIRITUAL
AWAITS YOUR EFFORT

Sight is natural, but requires practice to make perfect. In the same way, many of our natural abilities require training. Training is, in fact, a pre-requisite for seeing the full reality of what has always been, all around us. We miss the implication of the profoundly simple things, because they are so close to us. We lose the chance to perceive fullness when we are shaped by so many forces of cultural conditioning. The evidence of the negative impact of such conditioning is clear. How else can we explain people robotically doing things that bring no happiness whatsoever? A powerful conditioning of the self has taken place, and this conditioning often makes us think that we should "do" something that doesn't feel right, because it "makes sense."

A Taoist practitioner once told me, "If it doesn't build balance, it can't make sense".

Whether you are communistic or capitalistic, religious or not, do your views support a simple and holistic balance with nature and your fellow man? Regardless of ideology we are all human beings. Who would you be if you had just been allowed to be you? The real you. Where is this person? Can he or she be rescued? The shamans say, "Yes!"

In almost all human activities, practice and training bring us from a general level of perception to a state of fuller perception. In the state of fuller perception, we cannot believe what we missed *before* we *re-learned* naturalness! Spiritual insight is similar, but is in fact, more natural, and for that reason, is so easily overlooked.

If we learn to observe the process by which we overlook what is close and obvious, we will understand the need to "train" the body-mind. Training is a readjustment to our natural fullest perception – the perception we had as children. Psycho-social conditioning is complex. Not all conditioning promotes holistic health and wellness. If we don't carefully evaluate our habitual preferences in relation to holistic balance, we may lose the perception of our natural happiness. As a result, we often turn away from those things that truly support wellness, and worst of all, we may actually convince ourselves it's okay.

The conditioning comes from all quarters. Run away from one thing and some other conditioning is ready to draw you into the fold. Is it possible to live a life liberated from this conditioning, a life free of any ego trip in any form whatsoever? The shamans say, yes, but first we must rediscover our fuller functioning. Recovering this functioning is the path of shamanism and requires work, because the net in which we are ensnared is so tremendously complex. Ironically, the answer is simple.

For as much time as you had put into learning how to walk, you will need to place into your quest for the Divine. Anything less simply won't do. But you don't remember how much energy it took even just to learn how to walk, do you? Can you possibly remember what it took to learn how to walk? As much energy as it takes to earn a Ph.D., *at least* that much is required for knowledge of the Divine! The study is one of recovering and refining, not accumulating more mental junk.

And so, put in the effort and recover your naturalness. If you do, you cannot help but travel quickly your path of shamanism, your entry through the gateway of the miraculous. And as you travel, you will track towards the heart of the Divine and the meaning and purpose of life itself.

SUMMARY OF PART TWO

*E*ach chapter of Part Two sheds light on important aspects of the shaman's quest. The quest is directed to applying our full mental and physical potential in harmony with life itself. Because life is not man made, we are called to harmonize with the cycles on which we depend.

Although humanity should harmonize with life's balance, we are also unique in being able to choose the opposite. As the Old Testament puts it, humanity is made in the "image and likeness of God." On one level, this means that while we may harmonize with existence, we have the power of God within us – the power to destroy existence as well.

The shamans know that in order to be happy, we must seek our own vision. Finding our vision means coming to terms with our mental and physical gifts. Once identified, we then have to find a valid way to express those gifts. Expressing our gifts not only feels better while we live, but ensures good fortune in the worlds beyond.

Section two also offered true stories to inspire us as we meet the challenges of everyday life. The stories you have read in this book are true, as are many of the stories often categorized as "myth" by those who claim authority. Having walked both in academia and with the shamans, I now see that one must become a practitioner before one can speak of the practices. And the fundamental practice that must be completed as entrance exam, is the reorientation of ego to wholeness.

Those who write of the shaman's world without having undergone this most basic rite of passage can only offer well-intentioned guesses at best. Our ancestors lived in wholeness. The wisdom and truth of their stories emerges from wholeness, and it is with a heart of wholeness we must approach. Any lesser state subjects our understanding to partiality. There is more truth in our ancient stories than we think. Truth requires the wholeness of heart and mind.

Collectively, our stories give us a way to connect with one another while encouraging creative solutions to the challenges we face each and every day. One of the greatest errors of modern culture is the relegation of our ancestral heritage to imagination, allegory, or fable. There is truth in our stories, and we must not lose touch with that truth.

In order to reconnect with our stories, and in order to set the stage for the stories we will create, we need a daily practice. We require a means for keeping our quest in the forefront of our minds each and every day. Daily cultivation is the means to this end. Cultivation is made easier with a practice schedule. Practice helps us remind us of the basic principles while giving us the opportunity to develop essential skills. Such a practice is the subject of Part Three.

PART THREE

Basic Training

Parts one and two have laid the foundation of content and inspiration as we begin our own vision quest. Finding that vision means nurturing both the necessary insight and the capacity to manage the forces operating in our lives. Successfully managing these forces brings improved balance and ability.

Working with your vision is a lifelong process. The process never ends, and the work is never done, but the rewards are worth it. Thankfully, managing balance always rewards us generously. Developing balance is a lifelong process and is endlessly creative. Immersed in such creativity, you will find inspiration throughout life. No matter where you start, there is always a new way to apply your vision, and there is always room to improve. For this reason, the shamanic process is continuous and creative. It really *is* a way of life.

Throughout human history this "way of life" has been called by many names. "Tao," "Dharma," and the "Way of Grace" are but a few of these names. While the names are many, there is a single ethic underlying nearly all shamanic paths. Simply stated, the ethic is, "express naturalness while not harming another's ability to develop naturally as well." The value of this ethic is proven by art and science and tradition. Many shamanic paths work from this standpoint, and the results these paths achieve prove the merits of this approach.

Despite possessing near miraculous skills, the work of the shaman is not to impose his or her will on existence – though that is possible. In fact, the shaman's work is to discover and honor the seamless interface between one's personal vision and nature's ability to meet that vision. The aim is harmony, but it's not always easy. Troubles do come. In the face of adversity, the shaman may counter imbalance but aspires to do so in a way that generates compassion, understanding, and balance with nature.

The dance of shamanism is to discover one's true vision, and to follow that vision for the benefit of oneself and others. Discovery requires a balancing of the self. Balancing involves managing tension and relaxation within the natural range of psychophysical motion. The words sound complex, but the experience is simple. Nurturing the experience is what we shall focus on now.

Managing change is important and involves a learning curve. We must learn how to balance capacity, flexibility, and ability. It's quite similar to the journey from childhood into maturity. A child has a limited ability to manage mental and physical change. Because of that, children must rely on their parents. Naturally, as we mature, things change. As adults, we're called to manage physical and mental change on our own. As adults, we still need others, but the essential work must come from within.

Because each and every person must walk their own path, it's important to have a basic set of skills to help support our ability to balance our lives. Those skills are the activities of the shaman's tool kit. Applying those tools towards balancing your life is your vision quest.

YOUR VISION QUEST

*Y*our unique, irreplaceable contribution to the balance and benefit of life is your vision. It may be big, or it may be small. In most cases, a life's vision is a combination of the two. Discovering your vision is your vision quest. While there's often an overarching vision which holds sway during our lives, it is also common that one's vision changes over time. Just relax. Life will help you learn.

Let your skills meet life's need.
Don't be alarmed if the vision that worked for you as a young adult no longer "works" now. *Life is changing too*. We may need to build new skills in order to meet life as it is. Despite the change, there is a unifying thread: the humble desire to respect the precious gift of human life, abiding as it does at the crossroads of the creative.

Expressing our vision quest requires activity. It is a process of addition. Discovering the vision is, more often than not, a process of subtraction.

The process of subtraction is allowing the natural wisdom encoded within you, to exist hygienically despite cultural inputs.

The vision quest reveals the natural you, the one that lived before the pressure of cultural inputs and psychological impressions "told" you how to be. Before you were "told" that you weren't an artist; before you were "told" that you couldn't "do" science; before someone "told" you what it "meant" to be tall, short, fat, skinny, *or whatever.*

Before all the hassles and hang-ups is you

The vision quest reintroduces you to the best parts of yourself, the parts you left behind because you feared that they were not "mature" or "acceptable" to parents, society or your own image of yourself.

Feel your unhappiness, if you have some. Where does it live? When did it begin? How has it forced you to change, bend, and twist? What "acts" must you present to others in order to make them believe it's all OK? You will have more energy and more happiness if you stop pretending.

Would the five-year-old you respect how you are living now? The 10-year-old you? The adolescent? When did it change? Are you holding tension? Are you living a double life? A triple life? Go back and rescue the parts of yourself that are waiting.

You are waiting

Since the present moment exists in the world of activity, the vision quest mostly unfolds in the realm beyond activity – the silent space, pregnant with potential. Returning to that place, we find that the past has never left us, and from the guise of the present, totality is known.

The great deception is that there is any separation. The Great Lever is the fulcrum between the very concept of fragmentation and the burst of awareness that there can be no fragmentation whatsoever. Sacredness is held within that space.

The vision quest is your process of recognizing and realizing availability to the wholeness of being. The many shamanic traditions apply proven tools for promoting the integrity which reorients and realigns whatever needs healing.

Improving our alignment with life is healing.

Maximizing our time spent with this wholeness makes possible the healing of the past, present and future.

Healing this moment now, we change the universe in its entirety.

Releasing the stranglehold of thought and compulsion, we cooperate with life, allowing tension and relaxation as required by conditions. For those seeking balance, cultural conditioning and propaganda hold no sway.

As we release unnecessary tension, tremendous energy is freed in our own body and mind, *because it takes energy to restrain things.*

Sometimes the vision quest is exhausting, especially if we try to correct everything in a day, a week, or a year. While there are special communities that support such intense vision quests, the process can also be achieved more gently, more gradually. Which one you choose is up to you and the demands of your life.

Although it feels like tremendous effort is required, insight is a process of letting go. What requires energy is the tension of continually doing what cannot bring happiness. Why continue to live a shadow life? Harmonize the good and the bad, place it all in the crucible of cultivation, and allow the intelligence of life to balance you as effortlessly as she can.

This section will share effective methods you may incorporate in your vision quest, methods that will help promote a smooth and even exchange of energy. Wherever your vision quest leads, these practices help reduce stress and promote your ability to balance the forces of your life. The tools of this section support a holism, complementary to what you have learned so far. While there are literally thousands of shamanic methods, these few will support effective growth no matter where you travel. Good luck, and enjoy the process.

As we begin, I suggest that you create your own shamanic journal. Whenever you wish, record memorable moments along the way. The entries aren't meant to be about hanging on to the past, but instead to serve as inspiration. Journaling may occasionally provide you with yet another outlet to express some of the tremendous information that will come to you as you begin this journey.

Let's get started.

THE FIVE POINTS AND
THE NECESSITY OF CONSISTENT PRACTICE

*B*asic training involves the application of the five points of practice. Practice provides the opportunity to remember and experiment with wisdom in the theater of life. Making a schedule of this experimentation is important. Scheduling practice time is necessary because the challenges of life often conspire to take that time away. There will come a time when no schedule is needed, but for now, a schedule is useful. As the old saying goes, "from discipline comes freedom."

The five points serve as structure in which the practitioner explores the wisdom of the five elements, three gates, and the teachings handed down from the ancestors. If structured properly, one concise practice session will contain a review of the entire body of shamanic lore. Practice is holographic. Exploring life through practice, we gain insight and promote health. Applying those insights in our daily lives makes the world a better place. Perhaps there is no better measure of the success in life than that – having done your best to care for yourself and the world.

The five points manifest in the three gates and five elements of life. Here are the five points:

Recognizing the structure and flow of energy/consciousness in the body

Recognizing how energy and structure respond in movement

Recognizing how energy and structure respond in stillness

Recognizing the manifestations of interdependence, seeing the process of yourself and all your connections to all other beings

Remembering that life is not man made and for this reason we
even give the fruits of practice to grace, aspiring that our
actions may serve the benefit of others and that Grace will
guide us along the way

There are many ways to practice the five points. Each school
of shamanism does so differently. Nonetheless, there are certain basic practices that will support your full potential regardless of the
path you walk. The complexity of a practice session does not necessarily guarantee more insight. As with many things, the simple often
contains the profound.

Basic Structure and Frequency of Practice

The length of your practice time is less important than the quality
invested in the time you have. Generally speaking, 15 to 20 minutes
a day is a good start. Later, you may evolve the basic practice session as needed. Some people split the routine into a morning and
evening session. Do what you need to make your practice fit your
schedule. It is important to bear that in mind. Practice was made
to support your life; your life was not made for the practice. Still,
we should be realistic. Your practice must align with the goals you
seek. Practicing once a week can't resolve tensions that have taken
decades to develop. Be realistic, yet keep your heart open to the
miraculous.

At some point in the future, you may decide to formally study
with one school or another. Feel free to use these fundamentals as
an adjunct to training. The five points synergize with all methods, so
use them as you like.

POINT ONE: General Loosening
and Warm-Up – Happy Shaking

Begin by affirming that you are happy to be doing your practice.
Dedicate the benefits of your practice to yourself and others. Affirm
that by balancing yourself, you will be improving the balance of the

universe. Dedicate the balancing you achieve in your practice to supporting the balance of all beings limitlessly. This affirmation is important. Even if you are having a bad day, start your practice by acknowledging this motivation. Holistic motivation promotes favorable conditions. Once you are established in a positive motivation, gently shake and loosen the joints and limbs. Do this until you feel warm and comfortable.

During the process of Happy Shaking (as Master TK Shih calls it), when you find places of stiffness and tension, simply acknowledge the stiffness and accept that, in time, it will melt away. There is no need to *drive* tension away.

Don't think about *fighting* tension. After all, the tension you're feeling is a part of you that has become tense. There is no need to fight it. You can't fight yourself. On the other hand, you can relax, and you can heal. Be gentle. Let stiffness melt away gradually. In most cases, stiffness comes from neglect. Trauma and fear also cause stiffness. With careful attention, neglect can be corrected. In time, all imbalances can be improved.

Experience has shown that using a gentle approach is useful. By paying attention to and meeting your body in relaxation, stiffness will release, and we maximize the effectiveness of the practice. With correct relaxation, there is healing and with more healing, more relaxation. And with more relaxation, more availability to wholeness. Such is the nature of progress.

Once you feel sufficiently warmed up, move on to point number two. Of course, with this and all the five points, feel free to practice them whenever the time is right.

POINT TWO: Peaceful Quiet Sitting

Simply sit down in a comfortable position, and inhale and exhale from the belly. If you are too weak to sit, lay in a comfortable position. With the inhale, simply acknowledge the fact that you are inhaling. As you exhale, acknowledge that that you are exhaling too.

If additional thoughts come to the mind, let them come, and gently let them leave. Thoughts will come and go; there is no need to worry about it. If a thought is really important, you'll remember it later. During this exercise, just let your thoughts flow like water down a stream. Relax. Maintain a comfortably straight spine and *just breathe.*

As our practice deepens, we realize that each thought has an impact on the body/mind. As you tune in with the breath, you'll feel the effect that each type of thought has on your state of balance. Thoughts of anger disturb balance, as do thoughts of self-loathing or greed. By contrast, thoughts of peacefulness and compassion promote balance and creativity. In time, we become very precise with our understanding on the influence of thought. Gradually, we become skillful in how we think. No one wants to feel out of sorts. Knowing that, it is useful to pay attention to the ways that thoughts impact balance. In time, we begin to cultivate thoughts of benefit and effortlessly avoid those thoughts that lack sufficient beneficial charge.

Each thought has a ripple effect in our body/mind and in the way we live our life. Unskillful thoughts breed tension, fear, and confusion. Such thoughts are of no benefit to the life of the shaman, and indeed are no good for anyone at all.

As we sit, simply breathing, we release attachment to neurotic obsession with the ownership specific thoughts. Instead, we seek inspiration which complements our unique place in life. Allowing thought and grace to blend, we feel how thought and wellbeing coincide. Many adults have been taught to separate the significance of the impact of thought from our assessment of how we live. Such a separation is not only impossible, but leads to unnecessary pain and suffering.

When we do appreciate the balance of thought and feeling, little by little we will come to understand the process of how thought and the objects of thought impact our experience of life. In South East Asia this process is essential to Vipassana (Insight Meditation.) In the Chinese Taoist tradition, this method has been called Quiet Minding in the Heart. There are similar methods in the Middle

East, Africa, and South America. In fact, European traditions carry this method as well. The names matter little. Owing to the similarity among people, the benefits of this practice reach all who will but put in the effort.

The advantages of Peaceful Sitting benefit the body as well. Numerous studies demonstrate that "belly breathing" can relieve stress, tension and even promote healing. A medical study cited by Morris in "Pathnotes of an American Ninja Master", has shown that more than 90 percent of heart attack victims were upper chest breathers. It's a compelling thought. Letting the breath to sink into the abdomen allows stiffness to release and the major organs to function more effectively. Lymph and blood circulation improve, and increased organ efficiency comes from this simple method. Babies and opera singers also breathe from the belly. The Great Sage Lao Tzu once advised, "Can you breathe like a baby?" Breathing from the belly is a tremendous method, too often overlooked.

Spiritually, the benefits of abdominal breathing have been recognized widely. The Taino Indians named this part of the body the "tonal." The Japanese called it the "hara," the center. For the swamis, the navel is the seat of courage. No matter what path we walk, the importance of the belly should not be overlooked.

Practice peaceful sitting for at least five minutes a day. Eventually, you may work up to 30 minutes or more. Never forget, however, that the purpose of peaceful quiet sitting is not to become inert. Sensitivity and alertness must remain. The shaman must always be vital! And so, move your body when needed. If your back hurts, move around a bit, and then return to the breath. If your legs fall asleep, as mine often did, then just stretch them out and return to the breath. Little by little, the breath will relax, the body will become supple and your mind establish spiritual poise and be undisturbed by the waves of distraction.

As important as peaceful sitting is mindful movement. Mindful movement is the focus of Point Three.

POINT THREE: Daily Movement

"Just as nature is ever changing, so too should the human body move without ceasing."
                                                             -The I-Ching

Chinese medicine recommends that movement bring positive development to the body and be in harmony with life. Being in harmony with life means that movement must not harm the body. Movement that unduly strains the body is destructive to the body and impairs the functioning of the mind. Movement should harmonize with the body structure. Movement should develop strength through practice. At no time should movement break the body down. Every shamanic culture uses movement to improve the physical constitution and open our sensitivity to messages from the Divine. We too can make use of movement for that purpose.

In ancient times, cultural dances encoded multiple levels of meaning and importance. In many cases, dance served as a type of interactive history. Dance expressed cultural, anthropological, and even scientific theories. Embedding information in dance allowed our predecessors to pass on important information in a way that was easy, fun, and efficient. Beyond their anthropological value, cultural dances also prevented mental imbalance. If there was ever a danger in becoming too "heady," too abstract, dance brought us back to our roots. Our "roots" are the interconnection of spirit, mind, and body. China's shamans used dance at least as far back and 8,000 years ago. Similar histories exist among all indigenous peoples from all over the world. While dance is still perhaps the most common form of shamanic movement, it is not for everyone. Fortunately, one simple exercise can be adjusted in order to provide the benefits of dance. That simple exercise is the "Shamanic Walk."

The Shamanic Walk

Many shamanic traditions use this most basic form of movement as a way to keep fit and develop the lesser-known capacities of human potential. When dancing is impractical, just taking a walk or a light jog (runners may use these techniques while running), can do the trick. Whether you walk, jog, or run, the principles are the same. As always, consult with your physician to determine what level of activity is right for you.

If you do not have an aerobic component in your daily training, simple walking can be of great benefit. It can help tone muscles, improve lung function, increase oxygenation of the blood, and stave off the scourges of chronic disease. Countless studies confirm that even walking just a little bit helps. Naturally, when we augment our daily walk with shamanic insight, the benefits expand dramatically!

Native American and South American shamans used walking and running techniques, as did the African shamans. Specially trained lamas of Tibet were said to traverse immense distances by virtue of a skill called "Lung Gom." Activating inner energy with movement, these remarkable adepts used walking and running as a moving meditation. A study of their accomplishments is humbling. Thankfully, we don't need to be adepts to gain the core benefits of walking. We just need to walk with an ear to the Divine.

The Shamans Walk: The Method

If possible, walk for at least 40 minutes at least three times a week (and each day if you can). Improve gradually, working up to the goal of at least 40 minutes each time. If you can, walk in a park, or as close to nature as possible. As you walk, allow your pace to change with your thoughts. Switch it up! As your thoughts change, let your walk match their pace. When you suddenly have a flash of insight, speed up. When you feel a bit more relaxed, slow it down. And then, do the reverse. Notice how you can modify thoughts by modifying activity. There is great wisdom in that understanding. All the while, imagine that as you move, you create waves of harmony. These waves tell nature that you value her presence and that you are receptive to her blessings. The benefits of this are far reaching.

As you walk, imagine that with every step you take, good

energy comes up into your body through the Earth, and stale energy passes from your feet into the ground below. You don't need to walk barefoot to feel the benefits of this exercise, but try walking barefoot whenever it's appropriate to do so. With the heavens above sending energy down, stale energy travels to the feet for release. With every new step, rejuvenating energy from the Earth travels into the feet and up into the body. This is one of the macrocosmic cycles of universal energy flow.

Ancient texts describe the human body as a lodestone, aligned between Heaven and Earth. The top of the head is the positive pole while the perineum and feet represent the negative pole. With alternate, rhythmic movement of the body, a subtle polar exchange is affected. This oscillation promotes an even energy flow throughout the body. Many of the most effective mind/body arts make use of this simple fact.

Although there are many methods for tuning the mind and body, perhaps the most basic, accessible – and ironically, one of the most powerful – is simple walking. *Just take a walk*. It sounds too good to be true. Walk, and allow the rhythmic movement of the arms and legs to power the body battery. Keep the head upright, let the body become more relaxed with every step. Allow your breathing to flow naturally, emerging and withdrawing to the belly. Avoid upper chest breathing. The Shaman's Walk and Peaceful Sitting support one another. Use them whenever possible. Know that with each round of practice you are building balance and minimizing the impact of disease. *Dis-ease*.

As you walk, pay attention to your thoughts, but don't fixate. As with the Peaceful Sitting practice, let thoughts come and go. Every now and then, a powerful thought will arise and demand attention. Give it attention, and then let it go. If it's important, you'll remember it. As you walk, listen to the sounds around you. Lama Norlha Rinpoche once said, "Dharma is always talking to us." Dharma, the flow of life, is everywhere. Listen for the messages of nature. Be sensitive to the times during your walk, so that you may commune with nature. Whenever possible, speak with nature *and listen for her reply*.

A two-way communication with nature is essential. Communing with nature is really crucial for discovering the meaning and purpose of life. We are born from nature. And nature is alive. Nature is just as conscious… no, *more* conscious than we are. If we do not see our connection with nature, we make living this life so much more difficult than it has to be. Discovering our communication with nature, we reaffirm the integrity of creation and our place in that wholeness. It is from a deep recognition of that wholeness that we tap our full potential and make manifest maximal blessings in this world and beyond. Although very simple, the shaman's walk can be a great boon for those who plumb its depths.

POINT FOUR: Speaking for Nature

As was mentioned in "The Shaman's Walk," talking with Nature is an important practice and skill. When we actually hear what Nature has to tell us, we can carry her messages to others. This is what is meant by speaking for Nature. While our Shaman's Walk is a great time to practice speaking with nature, it doesn't need to be the only time.

Whenever possible, tune in with nature's design. Feel how she is formed, feel how she moves. Why does nature pull one way instead of the other? Why does a sapling grow here, and not there? Feel and think. Arrive at the natural conclusion. Listen to your heart with nature. Whenever possible, learn from the dynamic balance of nature. Notice her rhythms and the meaning of those rhythms, which reflect the mind of God. Notice nature in moments when you habitually do not.

While you are gardening, or on your way to work, *listen*. When you are walking in the forest, *hear*. Notice nature in and around your life, see. Nature is supremely significant. We are touched by nature at all times. *Feel that connection*. Without her, we cannot exist. Let that awareness strike you deeply. Without nature, we cannot exist. Venerate her lessons. She *is* life.

Take a moment, acknowledge the cycles of life occurring above, below, and around you. Each member of our natural family has a lesson to share. Each person is capable of internalizing the lessons of all of nature's kind. It's not that we need to meet each and every aspect of nature to do so, but when nature meets us, we should nod our head and appreciate the moment. Such humility yields tremendous benefit. Develop your voice as a human on Earth, and while doing so, improve your skill in communicating with the natural world – endless wonders await!

POINT FIVE: Reliance on Grace – Each Method In One, and No Method At All

Bruno Groening, the German mystic and healer, was fond of saying, "Life is not man made." What a profound statement of truth. In truth, the shaman's world hinges on this very fact. The insights we receive, the melodies we sing, the rhythms we play, and the movements we dance all come as a celebration of our place in the grand scheme of things. It is not merely an intellectual proposition. We are not just seeking something beyond the self as a diversion, self-delusion or game.

There is a Need

There is a need for our vision quest. The need is primal, and this need is crucial for personal and global health. Some traditions do not use the term "vision quest" *per se*, but the process remains. Ignoring the need for finding our vision breeds every form of misery. Your unique vision is your unique way of being you. Your unique being can fulfill your destiny and helps others do the same. There is no success when our vision lies unlived. Success is impossible when the results impair our humanity, our human-ness. Life detracts from our enjoyment when our choices violate our natural gifts. Life is a tragedy when our compulsions impair the ability of others to discover their vision as well. We must come to terms with our responsibility to live fully, while not adversely impacting the ability of others to live fully as well. Doing so, we find our place.

No matter how big or small your vision is, live it. Live it well. Your vision may only impact one or two people. But no matter the scope or size of your vision, your vision, just like you, is miraculous. Attend to it. I am reminded of the old saying: "To the world you may be one person. But to one person, you may be the world." What a miracle!

The miraculous is not only far away in some other dimension, it's also right here, right now. When we heal the scars that bind us, the miraculous can be known. Sometimes life teaches us directly, sometimes a teacher comes along, and sometimes the grace of God heals us in a way we would never have expected. Regardless of the pathway, the healing the spirit opens the way to the miraculous.

The miraculous is real and exists for reasons beyond our power to completely define. It is a tapestry woven by divine hands. We are threads in that fabric, intelligent though we are, but still threads of a larger, living tapestry of life. Because of this, there is a perceptual blind spot. And ironically, there is a need for that blindness. There is need to know that as individual threads, each person's vision *is* impaired to some degree by the space they hold. When large groups of people become blind, life becomes dangerous. However, when groups help one another to see, miracles unfold.

Despite the possibility of error, there is a need for our blind spots – they protect us when our egos run amuck, as they sometimes do. Historically, our blind spots provide reference point for growth. My blind spots may not be the same as yours and gently, intelligently, we can help one another. With individual awareness and a reliance on Grace, the greatest miracle happens. When minds merge in devotion to Grace, Grace counterbalances the limitations of ego. Life is not man made, but man can take part in the miraculous.

Humanity is fulfilled in its conscious reliance on Grace, and from that Grace all good human efforts are magnified.

In your practice, acknowledge both your imperfections as well as your strengths. Don't obsess, just affirm your wish to improve, and remember your connection to the whole. Recognize your birthright to accept the Grace that has been designed especially for you. Doing so will ensure that you use your gifts wisely. Using your gifts wisely, you'll understand why some do not.

In many cases, despite the improvement in your vision and voice, deep truths will elude your capacity to express them. You will not be able to give voice to what you feel in your heart. There is no need to expect that every insight needs to be spoken. The physical voice is for the technical; the spiritual voice, the sacred. "Actions often speak louder than words." Whenever possible, dedicate your appreciation of what you have learned to the benefit of all life. With such an intention, whether you speak or remain silent, your voice will be heard. Daily practice refines your vision and refines your voice.

While we can and should discuss how things interact (technical things), the sacred is secret and remains mute – almost stubbornly so. And so, while we should speak about things that need to be spoken of, some things – perhaps the ultimate meanings – are best left unspoken. For important reasons, the ancients only alluded to the ultimate meaning of things. Yet they left clues.

The ancients addressed the ultimate meaning in bits and pieces, songs and tales, poems, and pictures – a web perhaps, but not a bag. Things locked up in a bag become stale and lifeless. Our work is nothing of the sort. We must work and remain vital. The quest for vision is a path of vitality, a proven path leading to proven results, if only we will put in the effort. While humanity is made in the image and likeness of God, we are still called to do the divine work. And that work requires effort. There is a reason for that effort, and it follows close to the ultimate meaning of things. Discover why effort is required and you will find fulfillment, even if you cannot speak of it.

However elusive meaning may sometimes appear, this silent knowing is, in fact, the root from which the shaman's tree springs. The deep knowing of peace in body and mind is the cooling shade of that tree, informing us where we may comfortably rest, when needed. The tree, of course, is the shaman's lore and wisdom. This wisdom does not end with the tree, for the tree is life, and life is being. Abiding in this being is the root of bliss. It is a never-ending cycle.

Conclusion

The World Is A Better Place

*T*he world is a better place because you've read this book. It's not because of the book itself, and it has nothing to do with me. The world is a better place because, just by acknowledging the truths shared in this book, life relaxes, knowing that you see the fullness more than before. Life is safer. Life responds to the human heart. When the human heart is at peace, life relaxes with you. We are inseparable from this web of life, and life is fulfilled when each piece knows *how* it is whole. Even in difficulty, if we know the wholeness, things are better.

The greatest danger to happiness, the greatest danger to life, is when life itself believes it is set apart from all the rest. Life is made dangerous when an ego, enamored with itself, believes that its stimulation should occur at the expense of life. Such an ego is dangerous and blind. When blind egos run unchecked, the world we know hangs by a thread. Danger follows conflict, and for this reason all of us must take the time to build peace. Peace begins from within. You don't need to be perfect, just sincere.

As global citizens, we must hold ourselves and our leaders to realistic standards – not perfection, because perfection is a process. But we must expect a realistic attention to the quest for balance, while safeguarding the precious nature of existence. Such standards are realistic, sincere and validate the wisdom of the ages. Just as we individually try our best to cultivate balance, we must require that our leaders do the same. Those in power should demonstrate that they care for balance and holistic benefit. This is the ancient way, and it is honored.

The world is in great danger when people do not act in accordance with the balance from which we were born. I hear my Master's voice: "Do not change a thing unless what you replace it with is of equal or greater wisdom." Only an arrogant person would presume to outwit the balance of nature. Humility is key. Respect for interconnection is crucial, and Shakespeare's advice comes to mind: "Use all gently." There is immediate and lasting value in this approach.

Listening for wisdom, using all gently, with respect, we remember our place in things. We remember ourselves, our souls, and the intelligence coursing through existence. Perhaps we may even remember that we are whole. The masters say that even a flash of this insight, once in a lifetime, changes everything. Remembering, and then living that wholeness, changes the very fundamentals of existence. It is proven by both science and by the heart that nature can unfold miracles, when she does *not* need to be in fear of us. Carried within the relaxation of nature, there is a dispensation of tremendous Grace. This Grace is available to us all. We must only open the heart and not stop opening until that Grace arrives.

The moment we remember wholeness, both the feeling, and even the very composition of existence, change forever. This remembering and its aftermath is the greatest chance for humanity to express its full potential and to build a lasting peace for itself, and for all beings.

You now possess a basic tool kit for supporting your awareness and capacity to work with the wholeness of life. Regardless of the path you walk, the shamans will be there to help. Some will help in this world; some will be assisting from afar. Open your heart and receive their wisdom. Continue the shamanic tradition and serve as a peaceful warrior, a steward of life. It has been my pleasure to share what I know with you, and I pray the cycle of benefit will continue beyond my limits and reach all beings through all time, limitlessly.

www.ingramcontent.com/pod-product-compliance
Lightning Source LLC
Chambersburg PA
CBHW022021090426

42739CB00006BA/232